MASTERING MEGATRENDS

Understanding & Leveraging The Evolving New World

MASTERING MEGATRENDS
Understanding & Leveraging The Evolving New World

DORIS & JOHN NAISBITT

World Scientific

NEW JERSEY · LONDON · SINGAPORE · BEIJING · SHANGHAI · HONG KONG · TAIPEI · CHENNAI · TOKYO

Published by

World Scientific Publishing Co. Pte. Ltd.

5 Toh Tuck Link, Singapore 596224

USA office: 27 Warren Street, Suite 401-402, Hackensack, NJ 07601

UK office: 57 Shelton Street, Covent Garden, London WC2H 9HE

National Library Board, Singapore Cataloguing in Publication Data
Name(s): Naisbitt, Doris. | Naisbitt, John, author.
Title: Mastering megatrends : understanding & leveraging the evolving new world /
  Doris & John Naisbitt.
Other title(s): Understanding and leveraging the evolving new world
Description: Asian edition. | Singapore : World Scientific, [2017]
Identifier(s): OCN 1013474904 | ISBN 978-981-32-3491-8 (hardback)
Subject(s): LCSH: Economic development--21st century. | International trade--21st century. |
  Education--21st century. | Mass media--21st century. | Social prediction. |
  Twenty-first century--Forecasts. | Social change. | Progress--Forecasting.
Classification: DDC 303.49--dc23

British Library Cataloguing-in-Publication Data
A catalogue record for this book is available from the British Library.

The One Belt, One Road graphic, used under license from Shutterstock.

For any available supplementary material, please visit
http://www.worldscientific.com/worldscibooks/10.1142/10846#t=suppl

Typeset by Stallion Press
Email: enquiries@stallionpress.com

Printed in Singapore

Contents

How Thoughts
Became a Book

Building on New Thoughts

Ever since *Megatrends* was published in 1982, the question we have most been asked is "What is the next megatrend?"

Almost everyone, including us, would like to have a map, which would help us outline our path into a predictable environment called future. And with more or less imagination and interpretation information available allows us to draft a more or less accurate picture of what will be. The impact and success of the book *Megatrends* was based on helping people to sort out things they were mostly familiar with. And in due course take the single pieces of the present and form a picture of the future. At that time it was a guideline into the transformation America would undergo in the 1980s and 1990s.

Looking back to 1982 *Megatrends* it is not hard to analyze how its insights helped people to "ride the trends in the direction they were already going." The move from an industrial society to an information age, the most significant and most influential of the 10 megatrends, was well on its way and had already started to influence production, labor markets, communication, entertainment and social life. The stories people tell about the impact of reading *Megatrends* had one thing in common: it helped to recognize

10 trends that were already unfolding. The book made clearer what somewhat had been sensed: "*Megatrends* helped me to put the pieces of the puzzles together."

Megatrends was good news for the United States and for the world

Even though *Megatrends* was written based on developments in the United States and for the United States, people in other parts of the world (*Megatrends* was published in 57 countries) could benefit. The individual trends were making their way from the West to the other parts of the world. Readers followed the thoughts and reviewed and updated their own thinking. Getting clarity helped students, employees and entrepreneurs to project their careers and business strategies.

The transformation *Megatrends* described was fundamental, but it was a continuation of developments that were already working even though not obvious. In most regard it was pursuing something that was already in place, but not a complete rethinking. In most cases the change was welcome. And most important, the driver of change was and would remain the United States. Easy to accept for any American but also easy to embrace for Asians, especially the Chinese, maybe less so for Indians given the British influence. But the general as their orientation for progress and learning at that time was towards the West, mainly America. Even Western Europe, which never had a too humble mindset, accepted America's lead. From that point of view, *Megatrends* 1982 was good news for all.

In the 30 plus years since *Megatrends* was published the manifestations of the described trends became more obvious and the speed of implementation accelerated. During those decades as author and coauthors, we have dealt with the developments outlined in *Megatrends* in greater detail. *Megatrends Asia* described the economic rise of Asia, *High Tech High Touch* elaborated on the unintended consequences of the information age, *China's Megatrends* was about the pillars on which China, the challenger of the leading global role of the West, was resting and building. *Global Game*

Change, first published in 2015 in China, was mostly dealing with geopolitical change. Many of the developments had already been anticipated with more or less clarity in *Megatrends*.

New megatrends arising

The question what the next megatrends would be remained. But trends cannot be forced to appear; most so-called trends are fads coming and going. Megatrends do not come every second year. All you can do is to keep your eyes open, and that's what we did. And slowly, as we were traveling and observing the world, something seemed to move. It started as an indefinable feeling. Something was in the air. We could not quite capture it but we felt that it was something profound.

We started our research to get clarity on what was really changing. After a while we sensed that many of the developments had parallels with the Reformation of the 15th century. The Reformation of the 15th century over time led to modernity, the rise of the West and the world order we have lived with for the last 200 years. We started a manuscript and chose *Global Reformation* as its working title. As we went along we understood that just as in the historic Reformation it was also a time holding great opportunities. So our working title changed to *The Great Opening Up*. We continued our research and as it happens when you are very deep into a subject, one day it became clear to us: This is not just describing new megatrends. What we are witnessing is the path to a complete change of the global game. Not as the transformation described in *Megatrends* in 1982, finding its way from the US to the world, but parallel shifts involving countries in almost every continent and taking place in various fields and directions, feeding into each other, connected politically, economically, and technologically.

As in the 15th century, the change we are witnessing will result in a new world order

Our first approach to compare the transformation to the 15th century Reformation had pointed in the right direction. In the 15th

century it was the invention of mechanical movable type of printing that led to a communication revolution and changed education from being accessible only to an elite to becoming accessible to the masses. Cities were growing and affluence among commoners rising. But most important was the beginning of the fading hegemony of the Catholic Church. In our days the parallel to the printing press, the Internet, enables millions to connect, communicate and influence. Individuals and businesses no longer operate independently in their field of endeavor and within limited geographic areas, but are integrated parts of global developments.

Beginning with the Renaissance in Italy, enforced by the Reformation in the 16th century, the political influence of the Catholic Church and its control over education and science diminished. Until then the earth was taught to be the center of the universe, just as the Pope and Rome were the center of religion. Scientist were standing up against the wisdom of thousands of years: they believe that the sun was turning around the earth. The shift from the geocentric to the heliocentric worldview did not directly change the life of the average person, but it had comprehensive consequences, leading to an explosion of scientific breakthroughs opening thitherto shuttered opportunities. Nevertheless it took almost 400 more years before Darwin questioned the last domain of the Church, our divine origin, to be created directly by God.

In a parallel to the development 500 years ago, the hegemon of our days, the United States can no longer claim to be the helmsman of the global community. Its self-perception as the global authority is no longer unchallenged, its leading position in science and technologies challenged.

China, the driver and frontrunner in the parade of emerging economies, is claiming a stronger position in the global community and gaining ground not only economically but also in scientific progress, which for a long time has been the domain of the West. The self-inflicted crisis in Western democracy, the economic stagnation, the political polarization, all fed into the overall trend of a systemic change. The appropriate title was in fact *Global Game*

Change and it was published in China and India in 2015 and since then in 16 other countries.

Global Game Change was dealing with *what* was taking place. But it did not touch the question *how* to deal with it. How to deal with the complexity of change was moving into the center of our interest and finally led to writing *Mastering Megatrends*.

Chapter One

Introduction to a New World Rising

From Single Megatrends to Systemic, Integrated Change

In our previous book Global Game Change we laid out the new global rearrangements and its participants. And yet to stop there would not fully capture the characteristics and comprehensiveness of the global transformation that is taking place now. Within the next decades the individual megatrends will lead to a systemic, integrated change, a global transformation: politically, economically, socially and procedurally. And the speed in which all of this takes place is rising.

It is though one thing to capture and describe the characteristics of megatrends. It is another to understand impulses leading to systemic, integrated and disruptive change effective globally in all economic sectors and political systems. And it is yet another to focus on how to master and leverage such megatrends.

In many ways, enabled and accelerated by new technologies, the geopolitical matrix, the economic landscape and our working world is transforming. That makes it increasingly harder to keep up and adapt to all the impact. In the 1980s when Megatrends was written, there was no need to rethink global economic and political power structures. The West remained dominant and more so, strengthened

1

its position. But if we want to anticipate what will transform our lives in coming decades, we must be open to thinking in new arrangements in the global community and in many spheres of life.

Mastering Today's Megatrends

As we already showed, most of the megatrends we have to master today have their roots in the 20th century, where many of the disruptive technologies had their early beginnings.

We can start with the shift from an industrial to an information society.

In today's knowledge society, all information technologies are building on the technologies which had their beginnings in the 1950s. Nevertheless while the Internet in the past was mostly a social platform it is now changing the way we work, the way we produce, the way we understand economics, and maybe even the way we understand matter.

High Tech High Touch, which dealt with the need to counterbalance technologies with human response, has resulted in instant picture consumption, a world in TV, computer, and smartphones. How else would it be possible that the dignified *New York Times*, founded in 1851, 117 times awarded with the prestigious Pulitzer Prize has an estimated market value of around $2 billion while the Canadian media house *Vice* is estimated at a $4.5 billion value. Horizon media analyst Grad Adgate: "In an era of media clutter, they have really gone multichannel. A lot of companies want to do it, but its really difficult, because many times if you go past your core business, it can kind of implode."

Few media have managed to move ahead, or at least keep up with the change in how information is sought and consumed today. Media and public people feel the need to be present on all digital platforms. It is a world where the literary narrative is overwhelmed by a visual narrative. To be able to master visual narratives we need creative minds. One of the biggest mistakes in education systems is to cut down on subjects that support creativity like art, music and sports.

Most Internet giants have been founded and are run by engineers. But the most successful, Apple, could add the creative mind of Steve Jobs, to whom Chinese calligraphy was more inspiring than the beauty of perfect algorithms.

The globalization of our economies, dealt with in the chapter "From national economy to world economy" in *Megatrends* in 1982 has continued but the speed, interconnectedness and interrelationships have increased. What has changed is the direction of the driving force. While in the 1980s economic currents drifted from the West to the East, a strong drift from southern emerging economies northwards is gaining power, changing the geopolitical matrix.

The rising economic power of the Global Southern Belt has naturally led to a rise in its political influence. Understanding the mindsets of the emerging economies is not only key to the shift from a Westerncentric to a multicentric world, but also in the degree to which their increasing spending power can be leveraged by the business world of the West.

Understanding China, whose rise we dealt with in *Megatrends Asia* and *China's Megatrends*, does not only help to gain insights in its long-term strategic plans, but also facilitates access to its huge consumer market.

The introduction of the Internet opened the door to the creation of a new working world, which is still in its beginning stage. Now is the time to set sail to be able to leverage the potential of the new technologies.

The overarching megatrends are digitalization and globalization, interconnected and influencing and amplifying all other trends.

Highlights of megatrends

As our economies are becoming more and more integrated, we will see a greater integration with an increase of city-to-city and industrial domain relations. In social economic developments, the impact of a growing global middle class on consumption but also on demands in politics will be more and more perceptible. The contrasting challenges of mastering the demographics of aging populations and those of a growing young working force streaming into the job markets will become more apparent.

Economics/technology: Moving towards one global integrated system. Digitalization is amplifying the interconnectedness of companies and talents to develop new product and services. Digitalization in education will allow the delivery of quality education across geographical boundaries.

In geopolitics we are moving from a Westerncentric to a multicentric world. We are witnessing the rise of the nations of the Global Southern Belt. New trading routes will be powered by the dynamics of the One Belt One Road Initiative. New economic alliances are feeding into the process of the shifts in economic power and political importance.

The change in the balance of power in the global community will be the most resisted megatrend. While in all other megatrends, whether it is adapting to technological advances, the consequences of increasing interconnectedness and interrelations, solving demographic challenges, fighting for reforms in education and implementing environmental measures, nothing will touch us as strong emotionally as the shift in power structures of the global community.

Competition and Cooperation: The Churning Role of the Players

For the past 200 years, the West was the dominating region in the world. It was the driver of economic, cultural and in technological advancement. It also claimed the right to set standards in the business and in the political spheres.

One of the key pillars of the West's claim for superiority was that economic progress is only possible by combining democracy and a market economy. It is no exaggeration that this Western formula was the success model of the past. Its culture celebrated a victorious procession into all continents with Western lifestyle, Western business practices, Western clothes and Western food. And consider, when we talk about the West it is only 17 percent of the world's population. But this 17 percent is holding about 75 percent of the world's wealth. But this is now coming to its end.

The transition from the Westerncentric to a multicentric world will not happen without bumps on the path, nor will it happen overnight. The time frame in which we will be witnesses and actors in this transformation will be the first half of this 21st century. As in any major transitions, this shift will come with the need to correct and adapt to changing conditions. Europe experiences itself as the global moral authority. The United States understands itself as God's blessed nation and has been the world's largest economy since the 1880s. It is not willing to step aside and give China and emerging economies a free pass. Do not underestimate how dramatic the change is.

Assertiveness or peaceful rise

There is no way to talk about the new geopolitical matrix without analyzing China's new role in it. It is the key player in the global shift of power, which we described as the move from a Westerncentric to a multicentric world in *Global Game Change*.

When it comes to balance of power military might very quickly comes into play. For decades the US has been the only superpower in the global community. In the past 30 years the focus has shifted from US Russia relations to US China rivalry, all part of the longterm geostrategic competition between the two countries. And China has initiated a massive push towards modernization of its People's Liberation Army (PLA). And while China still stands for mass-production, its focus in economics as well as in military has been on quality-production.

In June 2016 we were invited to be guests at Tiananmen Square to watch the massive military parade to commemorate the end of WWII. While we were unable to accept the invitation, the whole media world reported the spectacular demonstration of precision and lockstep alignment, symbolically standing not only for China's increasing military might, but also for the alignment of the masses behind their leaders. Supported by the guidance of Chinese built satellites, its 12,000 participants did not stray more than a few centimeters from their assigned spots.

Commentators of the West on BBC news described it as "shunning creativity and innovation in favor of uniformity and obedience."

"China was the weakest in history when it was scourged by WWII," state-run Chinese newspaper *Global Times* wrote in an editorial. "But 70 years later it has grown into a miraculous global power."

Competitive coexistence

China is the driver in East Asia's geostrategic transformation and military modernization. It is on its path to regain great-power status. Its increasing global economic power and advancing military capability supports reasserting its geopolitical role and influence in its "three seas," the East China, South China and Yellow Sea.

China's assertiveness on one hand is met by its commitment to a peaceful rise. Its increasing economic ties with Asian nations, which will gain importance as China's One Belt One Road (OBOR) Initiative is shaping up, support its ambitions to establish long-term economic integration and prosperity.

Despite all predictions of China's hard landing and even its fall, China's OBOR will put the country even more into the limelight of the global community. And with its prominent position its influence is rising. Unencumbered by election circles China is able to hold on to long-term strategic plans and change course if necessary. China's success as workshop of the world in due course led to China becoming the scapegoat for shortcomings of the West, for missed years of adapting to the impact of changes in production and the working world, overlooking the building of new trading routes and new markets.

And while China is addressing its problems under the authority and leadership of an essentially one-party system, nations of the West are caught in party-political quarrels blocking decision-making processes and action.

Mastering or fueling the Crisis in Western Democracy

Once upon a time the Republican Party was a respected political power in the United States of America. Founded more than

160 years ago as a coalition of anti-slavery Conscience Whigs and Free Soil Democrats, it is now at the brink of collapse, at least in regard to credibility.

The US election campaign was dominated by the rhetoric of a philanderer garnished with the third world dictator-like pledge to put his opponent into jail once in power. Donald Trump entered the political stage through the side door of popularity, not capability. But he does have the capability to destroy future prospects of the party, which for long time was not even his. How the Republican Party can recover from its turn from first resistance to half-heartily embracing Trump as the their nominee is yet to be seen.

In the US discontent has reached a worrisome dimension. Arlie Hochschild, Professor Emerita at Berkeley, describes radical Republicans in her book *Strangers in Their Own Land* as "people who picture themselves in an endless line, waiting for their turn to come. While they are waiting patiently, they see people pushing into the line in the front of them, helped by the government. Blacks are preferred, gays are getting special treatment, Syrian refugees walk on red carpets. All playing the victim, while they are slaving away without complaints and the government rewards laziness."

On the other side of the war of opinion are those who complain about exactly the opposite. Bernie Sanders demanded dropping free trade and castigate Wall Street while at the same time spilling goodies over the have-nots — free college for all, public health care, high minimum wages and all in all a considerable redistribution of wealth.

A hollow man fooling a country

Did America get captivated by "a man in full" fooling the whole nation? The want-to-be President Donald Trump played the emotional game of "Making America Great Again" by calling on all the means to diminish it. "Believe me" won't be enough. Would he be elected would not be about being against the system but about how to reform the system. But the substance of laying out his version of good governing is as modest as his rhetoric is bombastic.

For more than a decade America has been struggling to find a new formula for achieving the growth figures of the past. Crisis did not start in 2008. The United States has today more than two million fewer jobs and many people need more than one job to make it through each month. Weak investment, and a slowdown in productivity are dampening the country's once strong capacity to recover.

No wonder anger and emotions are overruling reasonable arguments of how to *really* make America great again, how to achieve growth and revitalize in the US economy. It won't be possible without ending the gridlock of Republicans and Democrats eager to serve their ultimate goal of proving the other party wrong. As we wrote earlier, it is not the potential of America's people, it is the polarization, incompetence and stubbornness of politicians stuck in the political structure that are standing in the way.

It is a cliché, but we have witnessed a "raise to the bottom." The opportunity-oriented people's view though is that once you reach rock bottom you are standing on solid ground.

EU: How to Master 28 Mindsets

On the other side of the ocean the European Union despite the grandness of the idea is stuck in the fact that none of member country leaders manages to be servant of two masters, serving the interest of their own country and the interest of the Union.

Servants of two masters

Under the headline "Europe: Metamorphoses to Theme Park" we wrote (still with a more optimistic look on the US) in *Mindset* in 2006:

> "The 'Statue of Europe' has 25 mindsets and two hearts. The 25 country mindsets are stirring a mixture with ingredients that do not blend: tradition, ambition, welfare and economic leadership. Her two hearts beat in different rhythm, one for economic

supremacy and one for social welfare. Proud and ambitious each one wants to be right. But to reach either goal, they have to compromise, and neither side is willing to do so. Experience makes us believe that Europe is much more likely to become a History Theme Park for well-off Americans and Asians than the world's most economically dynamic region as it has proclaimed it wants to be."

At that time the EU counted 25 members. Adding three, Bulgaria and Romania and Croatia did not make it easier.

A rise against the "elite"

In many countries of the EU people demonstrate against "the rich" and follow the siren songs of right wing politicians like Marie Le Pen in France, Geert Wilders in Holland, Germany's AfD, Italy's Peppo Grillo, Austria's Heinz Christian Strache, the list could go on.

Western democracy we are afraid, has reached a crossroad. Being against the "elite" is not enough. A cultural clash supported by populist slogans, feeding division and widespread distrust in a country has its roots in a loss of identity, social affiliation and most of all, hope. We either will manage to find common ground on which to build and deal with the problems or will go the hard path and learn by experiencing the consequences of listening to nationalists and opportunists.

Mastering the crisis?

The first step for leveraging opportunities is to get rid of a recent barriers. That's true on personal and public matters. Looking back to China and Korea, their rise would not have been possible without cleaning up their acts. "Seeking truth from facts" was one of the pillars to support radical turns in governing. The solution for Western democracies does not lie in returning to autocratic governing structures as is taking place in Hungary and to a larger degree in Turkey.

It is taking down barriers and seeking common ground on which multiparty systems can build and not allow contrary opinions to generate breaks. It is to vote for different parties but after the election integrate the differences to a better whole. It worked for a long time and it could work again if we understand our responsibility in the process.

You can only master megatrends you identify

Solving the current crisis will take time and the world does not stop and wait. It should not keep us away from reflecting on our own standpoint and our own chances. The time of transition is the time to act. Despite all gloom and doom in the mass media stream, moving frustrated within "Likes and Friends," it is possible to get out of the negative current, detach from preconceived opinions and reevaluate your judgments.

In collecting facts and information quality media is essential and it is well worth to spend the money. But it is only part of the information mix we need. As we move forward in describing the transformation we will use examples and offer tools that will help you to develop your own news navigation system to make your own judgments, mindsets that support getting a realistic perspective of the first half of this century.

An old world is fading and a new world is rising

Whatever you have in mind, you can look at it with a positive or a negative approach. Even stick your head in the sand. We strongly vote for the optimistic view and love to quote George Bernhard Shaw who wrote: "People are always blaming their circumstances for what they are. I don't believe in circumstances. The people who get on in this world are the people who get up and look for the circumstances they want, and if they can't find them, make them."

With a realistic picture of the future, with insights where the new centers of activity and power are developing you can project your career and business moves. Our purpose is to create a better understanding of the unfolding global environment and to help overcome hurdles that may hinder you to make the most of your potential. *Mastering Megatrends* will help you to focus and harness the opportunities. The transformation is well on its way. We cannot stop it but it is in our hands whether we are in or out of the game!

Chapter Two

How to Make Judgments and Master Emotions

Do Not Build on Preconceived Pictures

"The rate of change multiplies exponentially with each coming decade. As a global society, we stand at an intersection of what is and what is about to be. How do we prepare? What do we need to know? What are the greatest possibilities ahead for individuals, nations and our world?"

"Crossroad of Change" was the theme and the questions raised at a conference of the International Women's Forum that took place in Chicago in October 2016. The awareness of profound change is tangible as well as the admission that we must get prepared to harness the possibilities. Nevertheless, even with the same state of knowledge people will paint very different pictures of what will be and where the possibilities are.

We have often compared the picture of the future with a picture puzzle. The comparison though has a major flaw. Picture puzzles have a given picture, which, no matter how many parts, only allows to be put together in one way, forming only one predefined final image. If we think about the future we usually have different parts in our mind that put together create different images. One can argue how much the picture in our head determines the final outcome.

But as far as our own lives are concerned — as much as we are able to choose, use, influence and create the circumstances we live in — optimism, determination and persistence will get us much farther than giving room to a negative thought and a pessimistic approach.

> Some people grumble that roses have thorns; I am grateful that thorns have roses.
>
> Alphonse Karr, French novelist

On a global scale few desirable scenarios might come true the way we wish. Therefore it is hard to draft a long-term tenable scenario for our lives. Too many factors can interfere; surprises force us to change course. And while it is already hard to outline a linear path for our personal life, of which we are in charge to a great extent, it seems almost impossible to sketch the future of global developments. The critical issue in both planning our personal life and anticipating the context in which we will live our life is to get the best information possible so that we are able to master the opportunities as they appear.

Adding to the challenge, opportunities do not arrive like trains in a train station. They may even appear as a disadvantage at first sight in an overall very discouraging environment. Almost 90 years ago Napoleon Hill, one of the first personal-success authors, described the various characters of opportunities. In his timeless bestseller *Think and Grow Rich*, Hill indicated that opportunities often appear in a different form or from a different direction. He wrote: "That is one of the tricks of opportunity. It has a sly habit of slipping in by the back door, and often it comes disguised in the form of misfortune or temporary defeat. Perhaps this is why so many fail to recognize opportunities."

Hill wrote his book to an American audience at a time when what happened in America was more or less all that mattered to make plans for life. And although America was still suffering under the economic collapse of 1929 and its aftermath, he was sure that "never in history have there been so great opportunities," but also warning that "those who are afraid of new ideas are doomed before they start."

Rearrangements do not kill prospects, but open up new scenarios

New ideas and new conditions can be frightening if we do not know enough about them. And, as we wrote in this chapter, fear is a powerful tool in mainstream reporting. "Apocalypse Now" was the headline in an article in *Der Spiegel* 30/2016. It raised the question whether 2016 would become the worst year of the 21st century. We agree with Mathieu von Rohr, the author that the world has somewhat come out of rhythm and that something is "brewing." But it is up to us how we look at it.

We can see change as a rearrangement that holds opportunities or as a threat that kills the prospects we are accustomed to Without doubt we are in an era of instability, as stability and global game change don't go together. Looking back in time takes away emotions and allows a clearer and more distant look at the chances and risks that occurred.

Learning from the Past

Most of us remember the change that took place in the year 1989, when after the fall of the Soviet Union and the end of the cold war the balance of power in global community shifted. It was the end of a frightening scenario of the cold war and the end of the economic competition between the ideologies of the Soviet Union and the West. It also marked the beginning of a short period in which the leader of the West, the United States, became the hegemon, the dominating global power. At the end it was the speed in which it all took place that took us by surprise.

Reading about the historical background and the efforts which for different reasons were made especially by the US and Germany, the 1989 events did not come out of the blue. Besides political strategies and planning, some companies were already speculating when and how they could leverage the opening of new eastern markets. Within one decade after the fall of the Soviet Union and the "Iron Curtain," which separated Eastern and Western Europe, in small

Austria alone exports to the East quadrupled. In 7 years it added 3.3 percent to the growth of the GDP and almost 60,000 jobs.

Compared to the relative small dimension of the opening up of Eastern Europe, the opening up of markets in Africa, Asia and Latin America and the rise of a global middle class are holding a much larger potential. Certainly we have to remain cautious. In the first euphoria of the new eastern European markets those who overrated the business opportunities, miscalculated the risks, and disregarded the difference in consumer behavior had to face losses instead.

Nevertheless it does not need political shifts to shake up established markets. The rule of understanding the markets is true at all times for all industries. Take the publishing industry, which due to its many local aspects is a relative small and manageable business. For years the former main source of income for magazines and newspapers were ads. Besides economic ups and downs, ads are closely connected to the number of readers. And for years readers were lost to getting information online. Parallel to that development ads in print have been drying up. The circulation of many print media declined. For years now we hear the complaints and the moaning, but what has been done to adapt to the very foreseeable changing conditions? Very little. Even though Internet advertising is the major driver in the amount spent on ads globally, many print media remained hibernating. No wonder it came as a shock when it was announced in August 2016 that Facebook and Google earn 72 percent of the world's online ads (excluding China).

In May 2017, Forbes warned that at least 200,000 software engineers in India's IT industry will lose their jobs over the next 3 years. The irony is that it is often the same technology, artificial intelligence, which first praises their innovators and then eliminates their very jobs. How prepared is India's once outstanding IT workforce?

Working against the inertia of the mind

Any business, local or global, needs a constant updating of the environment in which it operates. To remain in the game you have to be aware of the changing playground. There is still a lot of disconnect between the business and the academic world. And nevertheless, despite the common awareness of the importance informatics graduates have in the economy, Austria's Technical University is cutting informatics college placements in half. In rather inflexible education systems a lot of inertia has been built up and is working against switching to a much-needed comprehensive thinking. Without education reform incorporating the needs of industries competitiveness of countries will decline.

The future is a collection and combination of local and global events with much of it driven by new technologies. The more we understand conditions on the ground, the more accurate the conclusions and connections we can draw from the changing picture, the more we are able to determine our own path in it. This is true on almost all levels, from people to communities, from cities to countries, from a one-man-businesses to multinationals. A certain degree of uncertainty will remain, but how we deal with it is up to us.

Not too many feel like our neighbor Fernando Di Filippo, former New York lawyer, and founder and CEO of European Teleshopping company DMC, who takes uncertainty and hurdles as "the salt in the soup."

"The only certainty is uncertainty" has become a mantra. And depending on an optimistic or a fearful approach doors open or close. To some it comes in handy as an excuse for not being prepared and taken by surprise. It's a convenient instrument when opportunities have been missed. But as the example below will show to an open mind many developments are foreseeable. As mentioned before, not as easy as a train whistle that tells you that a train will arrive in the station, but strong enough to allow you to interpret and make conclusions.

Keeping up with changing environments

Collecting facts and possibilities of the present was the basis for the conclusions of *Megatrends* in 1982, focusing on the transformation of America. It was the basis of *Megatrends Asia*, 1994, describing the forces at work altering most nations in Asia. *Mindset*, 2006, was dealing with mindsets helping to identify future scenarios. And it also painted a picture of future developments at the time. One Chapter dealt with the EU and was titled: "Mutually assured decline." The conclusion was based on what could already be witnessed then, even though EU euphoria was still high. It read:

> "The 'Statue of Europe' has two hearts and 25 mindsets. The 25 country mindsets are stirring a mixture with ingredients that do not blend: tradition, ambition, welfare and economic leadership. Its two hearts beat in different rhythms, one for economic supremacy and one for social welfare. Proud and ambitious each one wants to be right. But to reach either goal, they have to compromise, and neither side is willing to do so. We believe that Europe is much more likely to become a history theme park for well-off Americans and Asians than the world's most economically dynamic region as it has proclaimed it wants to be. Economically, Europe is on a path to mutually assured decline."

The once almost unthinkable Brexit was only one, though a remarkable stepping stone in the decline of the EU. And while we can argue that Pied Pipers of politics used false promises to achieve their goal it is also true that the EU itself laid the ground for the anti EU to succeed.

It is cause and effect and it may well not always result in what we want to see. But that's not our point. This book like our previous books, is not about preferences, but about probabilities. And it is under that banner we drafted the scenario of the global game change.

Objectivity and Emotions

As we already affirmed, we are about to experience systemic, integrated and disruptive change in politics, economics and technology, aggravated by the fact that there is no central point out of which a universally valid worldview can be drawn. There is no absolute accuracy in how a situation should be judged. When in the 15th century the inflamed controversy over the geocentric versus heliocentric worldview began, the fiercest defended opinion could not bend the unshakable truth that it was the sun which was the centre of the then known universe and not our planet earth.

When it comes to an argument whether Western dominance will remain or be replaced by a multicentric world, it remains a question of the various angles whether one believes it will happen at all and whether it will work for our benefit or to our disadvantage. It starts with how we perceive change, which then leads to how we implement our skills and create a strategy to manoeuvre. Western dominance had its good sides, but now the West has lost its inner stability. Where and how is America grounded? What are the anchors of the EU?

Personal freedom is a great achievement. But as great as it is, it can be misused. Proving the other party wrong seems to have become the underlying guideline of America's Democrats and Republicans. In personal lives self-awareness, understanding who we are and how others perceive us, is a prerequisite for harmony of inner and outer world. Our reputation, as people and as countries, is defined by the environment in which we move.

Mirror, mirror on the wall, who, now, is the fairest one of all?

Snow White and the Seven Dwarfs, Brothers Grimm

Today almost everything is measured, but nevertheless emotions define the attitude we have. President Obama's vision that "America's best days are yet to come," may well come true. Not as a revision of the past but from efforts made now and in the future. But whether the global community received it as good or bad news depends on the emotional view of the US. The same is true for China. Its rise and increasingly important position in the global community can be seen as an encouragement for emerging nations and counterbalance to Western dominance. Or it is seen as a threat to Western achievements, economic progress and freedom of speech and human rights. On a domestic level the "China Dream" may be encouraging, but it needs to become clear to the Chinese what it is, before they emotionally connect and contribute the bottom-up drive it needs to come true.

The EU can become what it was aiming for, if it makes up its mind what it wants to be and sets the steps that allow people to trust it.

Africa's human potential is not smaller than that of other continents but it is by far not as realized. People who do not believe in having a chance are not even trying. Their hope is undermined by feelings of helplessness against the power and the greed of kleptomaniac rulers.

Latin America has capacity to get rid of what keeps it stuck one step behind its promising future. But even the most dynamic Latin American temper can be put in hibernation by mismanagement and corruption. It sometimes seems politics is the only profession where failure gets rewarded.

Technology, Economics and Society

It is difficult to get familiar with the changing picture today because we are not dealing with megatrends in economic, social/ political and technological fields, but with a systemic transformation shaking and rearranging the fundamentals in geopolitics and economics. All taking place parallel and interconnected, enabled by technology.

Before you back off in worries be assured that there is no need to do so. The only danger lurking is to hold on to yesterday's thinking, to believe we can hold on time and continue doing things the way we used to do them. It does not have to be as extreme as Donald Trump promising he will bring back manufacturing and coal mining jobs to the US.

Such thinking reminds us that we keep driving our car led by our outdated navigation system. Again and again we hear the voice telling us turn right or left and all we see in a dead end road or sometimes no road at all. It annoys us, but we have not yet taken the time to drive to the car workshop to have our car reprogrammed, which takes several hours. Consequently we can't really complain when we are misguided. It's our responsibility to update our roadmap. Not much different when we move through life with an obsolete picture of the global environment.

Some of the current developments worry us simply because we do not put them into the contemporary context or we are still living in yesterday's context. Looking back we easily understand how global conditions have changed and how the pace in which people were adapting or, even better, anticipating the changes, influenced their lives. Just think about how much the first industrial revolution changed the way goods were produced and the businesses made. And how a whole new working world was created.

Steam engines, introduced first into factories at the end of the 18th century, were the drivers of the first industrial revolution and had profound economic and social influence. Henry Ford mastered that megatrend in an outstanding way when he launched producing cars in assembly lines in 1913, initiating the second industrial revolution. The new method of manufacturing was not only rising productivity but also improving the safety of the workers. In the mid-1970s microelectronics led to another change in industrial labor. It introduced computer programmable controller and yet another profession, the software engineer. All of course made possible by electric energy.

Now we are facing the next, digital industrial revolution, industry 4.0. The term 4.0 goes back to a project on high-tech strategy of the German Forschungsunion (Research Union), an advisory board of the German government, in order to express the goal to introduce the forth industrial revolution. Boston Consulting Group estimates that the introduction of industry 4.0, or Internet of Things, will create almost 400,000 jobs within the next decade in Germany alone. That is contradictive to the very often-heard warning that digital production will lead to millions of job losses. One thing we can be sure of is a significant loss of unskilled jobs in factories.

Ready for industry 4.0?

In a 2015 study McKinsey surveyed 300 manufacturing leaders, only 48 percent of them considered themselves ready to master industry 4.0: "Only 30 percent of technology suppliers and 16 percent of manufacturers have an overall Industry 4.0 strategy in place, and just 24 percent have assigned clear responsibilities to implement it."

The future of manufacturers and suppliers will be greatly influenced by how fast and rigorous entrepreneurs will adjust their portfolios and respond to the opportunities and challenges presented by the digital revolution. The study shows at least good to substantial progress of preparation in the US (50 percent) and Germany (56 percent) and a surprising low rate of 16 percent in Japan.

China's "Made in China 2025" strategy outlines plans to upgrade and deepen the implementation of industry 4.0 in the 2016–2020 5-year plan period. Despite a memorandum of understanding to step up cooperation in the development of smart manufacturing technology between Germany and China in July 2015, the line between cooperation and competition will be fine.

The churning of a whole chain

The transformation of manufacturing through digital technologies is just one segment. Working life will be influenced by how soon education systems take the changes into account and finally start reforming the system.

Digital technologies do not only impact the future of manufacturers and their workforce. Distribution, marketing and consumption are all changing. Think about how much downloading music has changed the music industry. Or how the Internet has led to the demise of print encyclopedias. The list can go on. We will deal with its many facets in Chapter Six.

The influence of technology does not only have a huge impact of how we do what we do. It has strong social impact. It opens economic opportunities to people in emerging economies who until now were very much excluded from getting a share of economic growth. We spent 1 year studying social economic developments in Chengdu, Sichuan province in China. Many jobs were created because of new technologies and high-tech parks were growing almost like mushrooms in the woods. Technology enabled pupils to watch videos with highly qualified teachers when local schools could not fill the demand. Farmers who could hardly read were taught via videos how to raise productivity in agriculture, women were taught to sell their homemade products online. The list could go on. Without the developments and progress in technology the rise of a global middle class would not have been possible.

And yet we are just beginning a process of revolutionary technologies. Blockchain, which is an immutable, unhackable distributed digital database, is said to have the capacity to revolutionize the world economy.

At the same time that technology is changing economic preconditions and thus social structures. It has become a powerful political tool. Whether it is organizing protestors, or used as a communicating tool by governments and administration, it can operate as a powerful network for bottom-up and top-down purposes in politics.

And while we will deal with these matters more thoroughly later in this book, the comprehensive changes in production and work, the social/economic shifts and the way politics will work bottom-up and top-down are becoming apparent even after only scratching its surface.

The Transformation of the Global Community

We are creatures of habit. Not only in what we do, in how we live, but also in how we look at things. That includes our view on the global community. When we talk about the global community we are talking about 206 listed states of which 193 are members of the United Nations. By far not all of them would present the same view of the world. How we see the world and our country in it is very much depending on the domestic and personal environment. Apart from personal circumstances, the domestic picture, the relationships and status our own country has within the global community is shaped by political conditions and, though less so, ideologies.

If the look at the big picture of the past decades we see the world in blocks. Not long ago, up to the 1980s, communism and capitalism were the underlying ideologies for the two blocks, the West, democratically governed world, and the East, the communist countries. With the breakup of the Soviet Union, and the increasing capitalist performance of formally communist countries, the most significant differentiation was drawn between industrial and emerging economies. While in this book we will continue to use the expression emerging economies it is in fact not timely and often misguiding. Some countries including China have characteristics of both emerging and industrial societies. Qatar, which has one of the highest per capita incomes, is still called an emerging economy.

Opportunity-oriented or problem-driven

In addition, just like people, many countries have collective mind-sets, some tend to direct their focus on the problems, others are opportunity-oriented. China and the US are good examples for opportunity-oriented countries, with each country manifesting it in a very different way. Take foreign direct investments (FDIs) as an example. US investments are driven by market fundamentals, with attention whether a country or region offers a good return. Chinese FDI is tightly linked to strategic considerations in politics and long-term planning. Market forces come in secondary.

In its decision-making processes China has been willing to make radical changes in strategies (for the better and for the worse) if it seemed necessary. In the late 1970s, when China was practically broken and unable to solve its catastrophic economic condition it made a U-turn, a strategic, collective, centrally planned opening to the opportunities the once so condemned market economy offered. And while the framework and goals were set from central down to local governments, it gradually widened the frames in which its citizens could operate freely.

The US went a very different way. Its opportunity-oriented mindset roots in its history as a nation of immigrants. People who saw the opportunity in leaving their home countries and become part of a new world. A huge number of creative people who believe that they could individually shape their future and thus shape the future of the country. It was the pool of ideas, the efforts of countless creative and ambitious people who formed the "American dream."

Optimism paired with diligence and strategy

One of the outstanding opportunity seekers in the rows of countries is Israel. In the first 42 months after its founding in 1948 the number

of 685,000 immigrants outnumbered the long-established population. In its first decade Israel had to manage the largest migration
wave in modern age. The challenge did not only lie in the huge
amount of immigrants, but also in their mostly heavily traumatized
condition and poor education. The young country was about to
perish in its problems. Mid-1951 almost every second immigrant
lived in an emergency accommodation, unemployment rate was
more near 15 percent and inflation had risen to 30 percent. Seeking
every opportunity to raise money by a reparation agreement with
Germany, selling bonds to the American Jewish community, rising
taxes, cutting defense expenditure it created three projects: house
building, farm building, and finally industrialization all built on the
nearly inexhaustible energy of its people. Between 1950 and 1959
Israel's GDP rose 165 percent.

The early history of Israel reads like a sequence of overcoming
insurmountable obstacles. It was, as Ari Shavit in his book about
The Triumphs and Tragedy of Israel writes, "a practice oriented
nation, connecting modernity, nationalism and development in an
aggressive way," often at the expense of the lack of caution for other
people.

Switzerland, a federal directorial republic, with its very different
history, although geographically in the midst of Europe, refused to
become a part of the EU and saw its opportunity by becoming a part
of the world. With the lack of raw material Switzerland, which until
the 18th century mostly known for cows, sheep, milk and Emmentaler
cheese, has been has reinventing itself. During the 16th to 18th centuries the country began to benefit from the immigration of protestant
Huguenots and their diligence and ethics.

Mostly spared from the devastations of World War II it was in
an excellent position to benefit from Europe's rebuilding. But
instead of walking the path of stagnation of the problem-driven
European Union it has become the most innovative nation outperforming countries like the US and Germany. Nevertheless the EU is
Switzerland's largest trading partner. Swiss multinational companies like Nestlé, Roche, Novartis, ABB, Swatch and most of the
best known luxury watch brands stand for knowledge and high
manufacturing qualities. Switzerland ranks number one in the

World Economic Forum's competitiveness Report and the EU's Innovation Union Scoreboard. Its capital Zurich holds top rankings in the quality of living.

Ranking the rankings?

Judgments need a base, and in a world where we like to measure everything rankings of all kind are very much in favor. Not all rankings are as globally influential as the ranking of credit rating agencies such as *Standard's &Poor*, *Fitch*, and *Moody's*. And yet a country's ranking in various fields, competitiveness, business friendliness, quality of living and many more, are not only popular but in summary, do paint a picture of an overall situation. Nevertheless, different rankings on the same subject may lead to different results.

In the *Forbes* list of the "Best countries for business" Denmark beats New Zealand and Norway. All three countries have a small population (5.6, 4.4 and 5.2 million). We have to get to number seven, Canada with 35 million, to get over 10 million. The United States ranks 22, Hong Kong ranks 11 and China 94, South Korea made it to be 33.

The *US News* sees it a little different. In its ranking "Open for business" Luxemburg is number one, Sweden number two and Canada 3. United States come in at 23, South Korea 38 and China ranks 42. Denmark, the Forbes number one makes it to be number 10.

In the *World Bank's* "Ease of doing business" ranking China levels 83, Denmark 3, United States 7, Norway 8, New Zealand 2, Korea 4, Hong Kong 5.

Three rankings, three results.

Self-perception and external perception

Each country will most likely have its own picture about where it stands and where it wants to be in the future. Even within each country regions and cities have different opinions about their status and so do citizens and politicians.

And no matter what various rankings are telling, whether a country ranks high or low, each will look at itself and at the world through its own eyes. The same is true when it comes to the changing roles among the nations of the global community. Depending on the relationships to various countries the attitude will vary. Naturally the countries, which see themselves on the gaining side of change, will show little resistance fewer to accept that change. And its no surprise that countries, which see themselves as superior and leading, will face a lot of resistance to accept any change in their leading role.

We probably will not manage to remain neutral in all our judgments, but we can discipline ourselves to monitor how much a thought is based on facts or shaped by emotions. But once we have created awareness, once we are able to "judge our own judgements," we have a method to keep emotions under control.

Chapter Three

Understanding the Mindsets of the Key Players

The United States of America: The Stumbling Helmsmen of the World

How difficult it is to maintain the role as the leading global economic driver becomes apparent when we look at the United States. It conquered the position as the world's largest economy first in 1890 and still holds the position, even though the World Bank has declared China to be the largest adjusted to purchasing power.

If we look back more than 100 years ago, American representatives did not hold back to communicating their self-perception. At the World 1900 Exhibition the consul of the United States, Ferdinand Peck, boasted that the trade balance of his country was larger than those of Germany and France put together. In his book *The Tumbling Continent* (*Der taumelnde Kontinent, Europe 1900 bis 1914* (*page 22*), Philip Bloom quotes Peck: "The United States are of such development that they do not only deserve a distinguished position under all nations of the globe, but the first rank of the universal higher civilization."

After World War II (WWII) America's position not only as the leader of the West but also as the safeguard of freedom and progress

was cemented. It was in fact America's Marshal plan and its investment of about $129 billion (in current value) that helped build up
and modernize destroyed industries, rebuild bombed cities and prevent the spread of communism. In the decades after WWII, to the
turn of the century most inventions, technological as well as sports
and cultural life spread from the US to the world. Already in the late
1940s transistors, space observatory, supersonic aircrafts, the computer, and also credit cards, video games, diapers, and Tupperware
were introduced. The Internet and the new economy, social networks and the most innovative companies were founded in the US.

Moving from high-tech leader to laggard?

But now the once so indisputable leader in universal human rights,
economics and military power keeps losing ground. There are contradictive reports about America's shrinking middle class, and we
will deal with that matter later on. But in our own experience the
belief that diligence and hard work would lead to a share in the
American dream is in decline. We know from family and friends how
hard it is to accumulate wealth, and in this case we are speaking of
white, well-educated Americans. Much worse if we turn to African
Americans or Hispanics. No wonder many feel that politics is leaving them behind and turn to those who please and tempt with
promises that only miracles can make come true. Fear again plays a
big role. How could flimsy promises and hatred slogans otherwise
catch so many people?

Despite all domestic problems looking at military and defense
the US is still the world's superpower. It has by far the most aircrafts
of any country, cutting edge technology and the world's largest
nuclear arsenal and well-trained personnel. But when it comes to
directly deploying its strength the limits in using it becomes apparent. What hurts most is the loss of the admiration America enjoyed
for most of the 20thcentury.

For many decades it seemed there were no limits to setting new
and higher goals. But it is not the first time in history that a superpower misses the point where what has been achieved is not enough

to sustain the *status quo*. Investments in infrastructure, public transportation, social security, schools and housing were set aside and bailing out banks became a bottomless pit. On July 14, 2015, forbes.com, Mike Collins estimated that the total commitment of government bank bailout money was $16.8 trillion with $4.6 already paid.

It was the 2008 financial crisis, which marked the turning point in China's opinion on the US. In our experience people's admiration for the United States began to crumble. And China's official voice became more assertive. To be pushed off the pedestal as the world's greatest nation by a nation which only 30 years ago was dirt poor and backwards is disillusioning.

From the greatest to a great nation

America still is a great nation — but by most other nations it is not experienced as *the greatest*. Other countries, especially China, which sees itself as a great nation aware of its own progress in catching up, are rejecting such claims. There is no doubt that most of the technological innovations including the Internet and practically all ideas for social media were created in the US. Nevertheless the US has lost its leading position as the most innovative nation and ranked number five in 2015. Tiny Switzerland leads for the fifth year, ahead of the UK, Sweden and the Netherlands. The last time the US's annual growth hit more than 3 percent was in 2004, when GDP grew by 3.7 percent. A May 2016 PEW Analysis showed that from 2000 to 2014 the American middle class lost ground in almost all urban areas. The relative decline is not written in stone. It can be turned around. But the first step to reform and getting out of political gridlock is to face the facts.

America did not lose its human capacity, it has lost its political capacity

It is understandable that official America is in denial of its lost superiority. When we speak of official America we speak of two voices. Increasing polarized Republicans and Democrats are blaming each other for mistakes made. If two people aiming to climb Mount Everest would spend their time proving each other wrong in their strategy of how to reach the top neither would succeed. But what is so obvious in many examples seems to be so aloof in political reality.

Obama's 2008 campaign "Yes We Can" and his 2012 slogan "Winning The Future" were a strong aspiration to reawakened hope and ambition, just as was Donald Trump's "Make America Great Again." There is nothing that would speak against making America great again. It is the claim of sole greatness that causes rejection. And given that claim how can America welcome a global game change that does not attribute the US with political and economic superiority?

And yet the global transformation is not about losing or winning. It is about new settings in the global community and how to master them.

How would one judge the decision of the US Congress made a few hours after a passenger train derailed in Philadelphia on May 12, 2015? Instead of urgently voting for a modernization of the system the Congress decided to cut Amtrak funding by $252 million, further starving the struggling career. Traveling through the US there is no way to not notice the conditions of desolate bridges, potholed highways, and the general lack of an efficient public transportation system. Once ahead of most nations, its infrastructure is now lagging even behind other emerging nations.

America's saddest record

The saddest record the US holds is the globally highest incarceration rate. With a share of 5 percent of the global population the US houses around 25 percent of the world's prisoners. Most of them arrested because of minor drug crimes, such as the possession of marihuana, one million of them African Americans. African Americans are incarcerated nearly six times the rate of whites.

While fighting drug abuse is a concern most countries share, high obligatory minimum penalty in the US has led to the explosion of Americans imprisoned. From 1980 to 2008 the number of people incarcerated in America grew from roughly 500,000 to 2.3 million. The decision of creating private jails supported the dramatic increase.

The majority of African American's delinquents cannot afford to hire lawyers. Many of the assigned counsels are overburdened. Without changing the law and a reform of its judicial system America's sad record will most likely grow.

To "make America great again" takes the joint efforts of all involved parties

Returning to the American dream won't happen in the near future. Certainly not in a gridlock position in which the two political parties understand each other as threats to national survival rather than two interest groups competing and cooperating for America's best.

The *Economist* describes the Republican convention as "a four day lament for stolen national greatness," while the Democrats were "urged to praise their country for acknowledging lingering social, racial and economic ills as the first step to a cure."

For such a long time the US seemed to be almost untouchable by global economic turbulences. Focused and driven by domestic consumption its economy flourished and few average Americans' interests reached farther than their country's borders. Across the oceans it seemed was a world longing for the American way of life. Once there was the illusion that nations would embrace Western democracy and they would be able to walk in America's footsteps.

It is true that Western Europe owns a lot of its economic rise to America's initiatives and help after WWII. But the seeds fell on fertile ground. Europe had the Renaissance, the Reformation, the Enlightenment, the French Revolution, and Germany even though the catastrophic loser of WWII could build on its Weimarer Republik 1918–1933.

There was no parallel with tribal nations squeezed into borders never chosen. While it might well be true that the majorities of people in many countries would have wished for America's wealth and safety they could not reset their tribal, religious and cultural mindsets from one day to another. Democracy, as we experience it, has to grow and cannot be imposed.

Nevertheless the United States was, from a positive or critical view, the guarantor of Western dominance and, to a degree, working against authoritarian drifts. Now that Washington's superiority is broken, the temptation of authoritarian leadership is gaining ground, within America, within the Western world and, given the rising role of emerging economies, within the countries of the global southern belt. In the United States and Europe populism and opportunists are rising and nationalists only barely hide their ideological missions. America is losing power on open stage and as we already wrote in *Global Game Change*, a multicentric global community has to find its new order.

No matter how loud the call to "make America great again," resonates, the bright future cannot be achieved by a return to winning formulas of the past. Whether and in which countries the US will regain its position as a role model is a judgment made by the nations of the global community. America's influence as a defender of Western democracy and as an economic powerhouse will be measured against how it masters its domestic shortcomings and on how it redefines its role in the new global environment.

European Union: A Grand Idea Poorly Executed

It took visionary thinking to even imagine that nations fighting against each other in two world wars could unite. Not surprisingly the first steps toward such a goal were set around an economic goal, The European Coal and Steel Community. The six founding members were Belgium, France, Germany, Italy, Luxembourg and the Netherlands.

Europe was divided by the Cold War into Eastern and Western Europe. Protests against Communist rule in Hungary were put down by the Soviets in 1956 and led to a huge migration of Hungarians towards Europe's West. In 1957 the *Treaty of Rome* established the *European Economic Community*. This treaty was amended in 1992 as the *Maastricht Treaty* and again renamed to its current title,

Treaty of the European Union at the *Treaty of Lisbon* in December 2007.

Steps along the way were the dropping of customs duties when trading with each other, which by the year 1973 included Denmark, Ireland and the United Kingdom. In 1981 Greece became the 10th member of the EU. Spain and Portugal freed from their fascist rulers General Franco and Prime Minister Salazar followed.

Free flow of trade across EU borders

The Single European Act was signed in 1981 creating a free flow of trade across EU borders. A tiny village in Luxemburg stands behind the "Schengen agreements" which gradually allowed people to move freely without borders and passports. The United Kingdom has never been encompassed in the Schengen Area, and neither were Bulgaria, Croatia, Cyprus, Ireland or Rumania while non-EU members Iceland, Liechtenstein, Norway and Switzerland joined the Schengen Area.

The Euro, currently the currency of 19 member states, was introduced in non-physical form on January 1, 1999, and new notes and coins became legal on January 1, 2002. We remember standing at an ATM in downtown Vienna on January 1st, a holiday in most EU countries, getting our first proof that the Euro was for real.

The most competitive and dynamic knowledge-based economy in the world?

The EU was not only to create peace and stability but also "to become the most competitive and dynamic knowledge-based economy in the world." Dreams were flying high. It was never said but clearly the EU pictured itself as the challenger of the United States. In 2006, we wrote under the subtitle "Who has the right to run the world?" in our book *Mind Set*:

"Europe without doubt understands itself as the flag bearer of humanism that emerged as the characterizing spirit during the 14th to 16th centuries in Italy, in the cultural and historical epoch of the Renaissance. Philosophically humanism is defined as any outlook or way of life centered on human need and interest. That, in many ways is seen as the European inheritance and ideal. Style and culture is European."

"Clearly Europe feels superior to the picture that is painted of America, led by the French, who defined George W. Bush's America as a triple-headed Hydra breathing flames of imperialism, neo-conservatism and fundamentalism. The rivalry between Europe, which feels an intellectual superiority and therefore claims the moral right for economic and military supremacy, and the US, which is much more relaxed about its own way of life and certainly holds the economic and military supremacy, is inevitable."

Looking back our 2006 picture of the future of the EU was pretty realistic: "Sure, the European Union now has targets for emission reductions, renewable energies, biodiversity, and social inclusion. But they have little impact on economic growth, and in some cases, slow it down. Economic reforms are not moving at all. The social model enjoys such popularity that hardly any politicians speak against it out loud. Some do say it should be reduced, or made more efficient, but the model itself is hardly questioned."

"Economic reform is about improving an economy's productive capacity. Period. All talk about economic reform should be judged against this standard. As it stands now, Europe for the most part is hostile to entrepreneurs, just when it needs them most."

From 1996 to 2016 the averaged European GDP Annual Growth rate was 1.68 percent with an all-time high of 5 percent in the second quarter of 1995 and the record low of −5.50 percent in the first quarter of 2009 (data Eurostat).

This is how we changed and updated it for the Chinese edition.

Mastering economic stagnation with a failed idea?

With Bernie Sanders in the US, Marie Le Pen in France, Matteo Renzi in Italy, the phantom of a return to the idea of socialism is on the rise. But hardly any idea has failed as obviously and consequently.

It brought down the Soviet Union, the German Democratic Republic, and it brought Sweden near bankruptcy. Not to forget its most daunting example, Venezuela, where people are starving while sitting on one of the world's largest oil reserves. Socialism of the 21st century was the praise Nobel laureate Joseph Stiglitz attributed to Venezuela. Stiglitz as an adviser to retro- socialist Labour Party leader Jeremy Corbyn is as worrisome as his call as an "influential adviser" to Hillary Clinton who already was pushed leftwards by Bernie Sanders' surprising cuddling with America's youth.

Marie Le Pen's economic plans for the 2017 France elections were called "extreme left, anti-capitalistic and hostile to markets" by NZZ, the Swiss newspaper "Neue Züricher Zeitung." We like the way Austrian journalist Christian Ortner put it: "Marie Le Pen's plans sound like DDR light with good supply of red wine" (DDR, German Democratic Republic, former Eastern Germany).

Who would say no to equality, justice and solidarity as socialism is described in www.politik.lexicon.at. The problem lies in the gap between theory and practice. While supporting the weak is highly desirable, economic reality of stagnation and widespread exploitation of social welfare is the result on the ground.

To the surprise of many, with Bernie Sanders, who ran for President in the US primaries, Marie Le Pen, 2017 elections candidate for President in France, and Matteo Renzi, former President of Italy, the phantom of a return to the idea of socialism was on the rise. Marie Le Pen's economic plans for the 2017 France elections were called "extreme left, anti-capitalistic and hostile to markets" by NZZ, the highly repudiated Swiss newspaper "Neue Züricher Zeitung." We like the way Austrian journalist Christian Ortner put it: "Marie Le Pen's plans sound like DDR light with good supply of red wine" (DDR, German Democratic Republic, former Eastern Germany).

In all of that we have to keep in mind that when we speak of socialism, people in various countries will have different understanding of how to define it. And depending on where we turn to, we can see success and failure. It brought down the Soviet Union, the German Democratic Republic, and it led Sweden near bankruptcy. Who would say no to equality, justice and solidarity as socialism is described in politik.lexicon.at. The problem lies in the gap between theory and practice. While supporting the weak is highly desirable, economic reality of stagnation and widespread exploitation of social welfare in Western countries is often the result on the ground.

Socialism of the 21st century was the praise Nobel laureate Joseph Stiglitz attributed to Venezuela. If we look at the country now it became one of the most daunting examples with people starving while the country is sitting on one of the world's largest oil reserves.

If we turn to China the picture changes dramatically. What the world could watch over the past decades is an unprecedented economic success story. And while China holds socialism high, it gave it its special definition of "socialism with Chinese characteristics." The creation of a social market economy based on Chinese conditions includes constant adaptation to changing conditions. This is one of the large strengths of China, to be able to apply its interpretation of socialism with a strong attention to local conditions in its provinces.

Contrary to China, in the EU countries attention to local politics and domestic party-political considerations are often standing in the way of reforms, thus creating one of the largest challenges to the soon-only 27 countries of the European Union.

The largest hurdle of the future of the EU remains the conflict of national interests

The EU is at a crossroad. Shaken by the once unthinkable BREXIT, economic stagnation, the never ending crisis of the currency union, the refugee crisis, the threat of a German and Italian banking crisis, rules that are too rigid to support integration and the increasing gap between the richer north and the troubled southern member countries. Talks about the possible danger of an Italian exit will hardly lead to the institutional reforms necessary to solve Italy's problems under the conditions of the EU currency Union. Compared to the year 2008 Italy's 2015 GDP showed a decline of 7 percent, unemployment rate of 12 percent and its employment factor was

57 percent. If we compare it with Germany's 6 percent GDP growth between 2008 and 2015, an unemployment rate of 4.7 and an employment factor of 76 percent, one can understand the worry. Italy's choice to remain in the Euro will hold up as long as the fear of leaving is stronger than the troubles of staying.

"Without a restoration of the monetary capacity to act on national levels, or, as an alternative, the agreement of the North to a redistribution in favour of the South, the transformation of the Mediterranean areas into a poorhouse will continue, bearing the already visible consequence of a crack. Whether at that time Europe will be already dead or still in coma will not be in anyone's interest" (DIE ZEIT, October 13, 2016, quote Wolfgang Streeck, former Director of the Max Plank Institute). Europe's problems are to a great extent home-made. And they were foreseeable. Looking back at January 2002 and an article of the German magazine *Bilanz* shows that they were foreseeable: "Whether what many do not want (the EU), will end in the United States of Europe, and whether nation states will hand over competence inwards while playing sovereignty outwards, is not of economic importance. It is though of importance that a shared currency policy is demanding common economic policies and adequate regional clearing mechanisms. The first has been realised marginally, the later not at all."

The EU's plan of a bonding element composed by interest policy yielded to the European Central Bank (ECB) combing with the strict convergence criteria of the Maastricht Treaty clearly they failed. The Maastricht Treaty has been ignored and shared interest policy intensified discrepancies between booming and weak economies.

Conditions got worse when admission criteria were disregarded just to get southern European countries into the boat. Just as in the US the roots of the problems lie in the lack of reforms, election-driven thinking of politicians and political parties, and the incongruity of different economic, social and cultural positions of the EU members states. The situation is serious, but in theory not without a way out.

Trust and confidence reached a low point with *old guard* Jean-Claude Junckers's complacent statement in the German magazine

Der Spiegel: "We decide, put it into the room, wait some time to see what happens. If there is no big screaming and no rebellion, because most don't even get what was decided, we continue step by step — until there is no point of return."

That's what people have enough of.

Europe's migration crisis

Pride holds against admitting mistakes made, and election-driven thinking combined with self-serving interests of many politicians leaves dealing with necessary reforms ever to succesive governments.

While Europe's economic problems were enough to keep its representatives busy, the migration crisis added another challenge, fear. Fear is one of the most nourishing grounds for populists to place their messages: fear of labor displacements and fear of terrorist attacks. Terrible incidents of Paris, Brussels and Nice have proven that the fear is not causeless. Yet seen through a risk analysis, the chance to be hit by a terrorist attack is much smaller than being a victim in a traffic accident. Publishing the rising numbers of people entering Europe on different routes from Northern Africa and South Sahara Africa is feeding concerns as well as the cluelessness of the EU on how to effectively deal with it. From 2013 to May 2016 the number increased by 40 percent. Frontex, the EU's external border force, estimated the number of migrants across Europe to more than 1,800,000 people. But put in relation to the population of more than 725 million it is not even three per million of the population.

And yet especially Germany and France are already used to Muslim citizens. Turkish immigrants have the highest share in Germany, while foreign-born Muslims in France are a relict of its colonial days. If we look at the percentage of Muslims living in European countries France and Germany lead in absolute numbers, each with more than 4.7 million, but if we look at the percentage tiny Cyprus leads with 25.3 percent of its population, followed by Bulgaria with 13.7 percent.

What really counts is how well immigrants are integrated. Mistakes, ignorance and the delusive comfort of kicking the can down the road have led to a dangerous grouping of frustrated Muslims embraced by the open arms of radicalized Muslim refugees.

We can look at it from the dark side and see Europe caught in a guerrilla war or we can act and see that what on first sight is a huge problem also shows potential when handled differently. Europe is aging dramatically. Germany claims that 62 percent of companies are not able to fill skilled jobs. Small- and middle-size companies estimate that around 360,000 jobs are vacant. While 85 percent would be willing to hire refugees, bureaucracy and a lack of language skills stand in the way. As we wrote in *Global Game Change*, the key lies in the two big E's: Education and Economy. Education is one of the lenses through which we look at the world and our life in it. The ways millions of uneducated people in poor countries judge their chances in life differ greatly from those lucky enough to have had a good education. Educated people are most likely to spot the opportunities globalization offers to the country where they live. And they are less susceptible to being recruited by religious fundamentalist or guerilla groups.

Jean-Claude Junckers, a Junker or noble man of the old boy club, and usually not shy of self-satisfied attitude, in his State of the Union speech on September 14, 2016, at the European Commission, admitted that "the European Union is at least in part, facing an existential crisis." Martin Schulz, President of the European Parliament, repeated Junckers' warning words: "We are at a conjunction for Europe's citizens, for our Member States, and for the European Union as a whole." And Schulz called on Britain to not weaken the EU.

In a letter to the 27 governments Donald Tusk, President of the European Council wrote: "People in Europe want to know if the political elites are capable of restoring control over events and processes which overwhelm, disorientate and sometimes terrify them. Today many people, not only of the UK, think that being part of the European Union stands in the way of stability and security."

And, we must add, of economic growth.

China: The Rejuvenation of the Middle Kingdom

The most controversial of the country among the key global players is China. And, we must add, still the least known and least understood. That does not keep people away from having strong opinions about the country and its leaders.

Many things well known in the US and Europe are kept secret in China. The private lives of Xi Jinping and Li Keqiang as well that of other leading politicians are hardly known. Decision-making processes appear orchestrated, arguments and opposite views are never discussed in public. The implementation of rule of law is still lagging behind. The lack of transparency does not build trust in China. But despite all that China had the most rapid economic rise a country of this size has ever achieved in history.

Nevertheless we hear and read about its coming collapse, each decline in industrial production or GDP growth is seen as a sign towards it. Rising wages, heavy pollution and increasing inequality are adding to the problems. Reports about corruption and violation of human rights are filling many pages of Western newspapers and magazines. And yet China's GDP is still growing, its infrastructure more up-to-date than in most Western countries, and the government continues to have high approval rates. If one looks at the Pew research of global acceptance of China by other nations on average 49 percent are favorable to China, and 32 percent unfavorable. If we have a look at the judgments on how China's growing economy is influencing their own country the overall view is 27 percent bad and 53 percent good, although with wide various. Italy leads the negative judgments with 75 percent bad while Kenya is the frontrunner in a positive view with 80 percent good. But whether it is a personal or a national view, it is mostly subjective and short term. So how can we describe China in an overall, and, as much as possible, neutral way?

China is not a monolith

First of all, just as the US and Europe, China is not a monolith. The best comparison might be the 50 States of the US, which show many differences. China is divided into 22 provinces, five autonomous regions, such as Tibet and Inner Mongolia, and four directly controlled municipalities, such as Chongqing, Beijing, Tianjin. Municipalities and Special Administrative Regions have been given special governmental status and increased levels of autonomy.

How China is divided geographically or administratively is interesting, but much more important is to understand how China thinks. And China thinks differently. From a Chinese point of view, and here we speak about the majority of the Chinese people, what really counts is that their government maintains economic progress and economic freedom.

China and the question of democracy

It is a misinterpretation of the West that the wish of most Chinese is to establish Western democracy.Chinese will agree with Americans and Europeans that freedom is of high value. But freedom means different things to different people. Chinese thinking is very much influenced by two fundamental requirements: social order and harmony. Social order and harmony were central to the teachings of Confucius who believed that it was only order that could provide true freedom for people. This is similar to team sports, where rules set the condition for freedom in playing. In the same way, an orderly society establishes the context for people to act with freedom. Order in the Chinese way of thinking does not oppress freedom, but defines the room to maneuver.

Freedom for Americans means the opportunity to determine how they live their lives, unfettered by arbitrary actions of others. This view is shared by most of the Western world where the rights of the individual are a major pillar of the society. From this perspective, what the West understands as the freedom of choice by the individual, with limited social and legal contexts established by each society, leads to continuing preoccupation with who is right and who is wrong. Indeed, many in the West believe that it is the contentiousness and discord that leads to breakthroughs, new ideas and innovation. But such conflict and disharmony do not fit the Chinese mentality, especially in such serious matters as governance. The differences in thinking are hard to overcome. We do not have to agree, we just have to accept the differences.

Regaining their country and their lives

Our Chinese friend Vigil once summarized: "Mao gave us back our country, Deng Xiaoping gave us back our lives." How can we understand such statement? Even for us, as we have travelled China for many years and talked with many Chinese of various social and educational levels, it took years to get a feeling of what is meant by that saying. Mao is attributed to have freed China after 100 years of humiliation, which began in the mid-20th century and ended when the People's Republic of China was founded. China had its territory back but to the average Chinese very tough 30 years would follow. Economic freedom and the opportunity to shape their lives individually is attributed to Dung Xiaoping and his "reform and opening up of" initiative of China.

Many in the West cannot understand why Mao's picture still overlooks Tiananmen Square when practically all Chinese know about the enormous loss of life Mao's strategic errors and political campaigns led to. There are many Mao fanatics who blame circumstances and Mao's advisers for the starvations and killings, but even those who blame it on Mao remain thinking that without him China would not have become a sovereign country. And that's why they still hold him high. From a party political standpoint he never left any doubt that the Communist Party of China (CPC) is the sole governing party. China forgives strategic and economic errors, but never party-political aberrations.

While this in Western eyes is hard to understand, within the Chinese group-oriented society maintaining order and stability is of highest importance. This brings us to another key difference in Chinese/Western thinking. The West is a so-called universalistic society, which believes that there are certain "truths" or values that are self-evident and part of the basic human condition. China and other cultures are what is called "particularistic" and they adopt the belief that what is right for me is right for me and what is right for you is right for you. If you are from a group-oriented society, however, where loyalty is first to the group and then to the individual, you of course would believe that your way is the right way for you and that others should stay out of your affairs. In other words, each particular society determines what is best for them based on their own needs. Most individualistic countries tend to be universalistic and most group-oriented societies tend to be particularistic.

A Turning Point in China's Feelings

While it is not advisable to allot attributes to entire groups or countries, there is nevertheless a mood one can feel. We have experienced the changing overall sentiments in the US and Europe. And we felt the changing mood in China. And while China as we already wrote is gaining assertiveness, it is at the same time increasing its efforts to win hearts and minds with soft power campaigns. The reason is very simple: emotional judgments hardly change because of rational arguments. That's true in politics, business and in private life. To get access to the minds of the people you have to open their hearts.

We are no messengers of the Chinese government. But we do feel the need for adjusting a picture that often shows just one side of the coin.

When it comes to making a point on sensitive matters, metaphors are an unagitated way of making a point, allowing people to make their own conclusions. When we talk to Western audiences, it is often not easy to overcome prejudice about China. Rational arguments do not take down emotional barriers.

Evaluating triggers emotions

For some years now, when we want to achieve a better understanding of China, we benefit from the fortitude of a Chinese high school student. A 17-year-old boy, whom we met in Chongqing, when we were invited to talk about China's future at his high school. About 500 students were in the auditorium, while about 4,500 more could watch via video in their classrooms. A big sign announced us as futurists who could tell the students all they wanted to know. To get a feeling about what would be best for us to talk about later, we first asked them to tell us what was really important to them.

It was quiet until a boy in the third row slightly raised his hand. It seemed to us that he was not sure, should he ask his question, or shouldn't he? We smiled at him and after a little pause he said in a somewhat trembling voice: "I love a girl — but she does not love me."

Here he was, standing up and reaching out for a love he felt was not returned. It was, we sensed later, like China reaching out to the Western world, and so often being turned down. To us the key in the boy's story as well as in telling China's story was to get a better understanding. In many of our talks about China the boy's story became the emotional bridge to our audience.

While we still sometimes use the story, the background is not the same. China is still reaching out, but China's emotional approach to the repulsing Western world has altered. Its self-perception and self-confidence has changed. And so did China's view of the Western world. As we wrote, the significant turning point was the 2008 global financial crisis. Looking at the West from afar, it was in a way an unmasking of the West revealing the weaknesses of the system and in due course, the difficulties to implement necessary reforms. China was able to master the crisis well and continued its path of moving up the GDP hierarchy. Before too long it will be at its top. At the same time China has moved from the fringe of the global community to be a central player in global governance. China no longer courts to be loved; it wants to be respected for what it is.

In light of these developments the 2016 G20 meeting in Hangzhou has been another milestone in China's new positioning. G20 members represent around 90 percent of the world's population, and about 75 percent of the global GDP. In this group, although not in a declared role, China also represents the interests of the countries we collectively call the Global Southern Belt, even though only eight of them (Argentina, Brazil, India, Indonesia, Korea, Mexico, Saudi Arabia, South Africa and Turkey) are members. The title of the speech of China's President Xi confirmed China's changing self-perception: "A new starting point for China's development — a new blueprint for Global growth."

The theme for the meeting was "Towards an innovative, invigorated, interconnected and inclusive world economy." And it should lead to "a course of China and the world embracing each other" as President Xi put it in his opening speech.

To sustain stability China's top-down and bottom-up forces must be kept in balance

There is an overall mood of renewal of a common spirit. A starting point that very much carries President Xi's handwriting. Much of what has been done domestically is welcomed by many, especially fighting corruption. But to quite a number of people who are involved in decision-making processes the "cleaning period" has led to stagnation. People have become afraid of making decisions. There is uncertainty of what to do and what to leave. At the same time a new generation is entering the job market. They are linked with each other and linked with the world. They are proud of China but they also have much higher demands than their parents and grandparents. China has benefitted from the parallel of being guided within the goals and frames set by the Communist Party and the freedom to achieve personal goals within that frame.

In *China's Megatrends* we described China's governing system that way: "The most important, most delicate, and most critical pillar on which the sustainability of the new Chinese society rests is balancing its top-down and bottom-up forces. Keeping the equilibrium is the key to China's sustainability, and it is the key to understanding China's political self-concept."

"The Chinese leadership holds on to the Communist Party, and the Communist Party of China (CPC) holds on to its command and control in governing the country — but the concept of what command and control mean has changed radically over the last 30 years. The party has changed from an arbitrary top-down autocracy to a functioning one-party leadership with strong bottom-up participation, a vertically organized democratic society with increasing transparency in making and executing decisions."

It seems that the frame to maneuver has become tighter in the past years. Guiding more than 1.3 billion people into the next stage of development is an extraordinary task. In such a case it is understandable that the pendulum that keeps the momentum swings out too much in one direction. But in the longer run it will be a break. Creativity needs its space. Its not bureaucracy and linear thinking, which brings forth inventions and innovations, but an environment that encourages imagination and entrepreneurship.

The other side of that coin is that in mastering megatrends neither enterprises nor countries can afford postponing decision-making processes. The efficiency of its autocratic governing model does give China a competitive advantage when it comes to achieving its goal of moving from "trailing the footsteps of others to getting a step ahead of others." One example is its latest achievement of launching the world's first quantum science satellite into space.

Xi Jinping made it clear that there is an awareness of the urgency in getting the economy right and that economic restructuring to a supply-side reform is in a critical stage when he said: "If we hesitate in making decisions and do things half way, we will lose this rare opportunity." What is true in the overall economy is true and applied for technological advancements.

China's growing desire for meaning

China's communist party is not only challenged in implementing economic and ecologic reforms but also in dealing with the domestic and global competition putting people under enormous pressure to succeed. The number of students in high schools and universities suffering psychological disturbances is rising. At the many talks we gave at high schools and university achieving high goals and meeting the expectations of family, teachers and society was the overwhelming concern of the young students. In addition there is an increasing search for meaning: How do I find out who I really am when I do not even have time enough to sleep?

China has been in transformation for more than 30 years, and the process has not yet come to a halt. There is a lot at risk. And only the Chinese themselves can work it out.

And they will work it out with a mostly optimistic view.

While in a 2016 Pew research most of the nations believe that the world is a dangerous place, the Chinese stood out. They have overwhelming confidence in their own country and they overwhelmingly believe "is the rising start in the international firmament." Chinese judge China's involvement in the global economy as good as it provides the country with new markets and opportunities for growth. By our experience this is also true in how they see their personal future.

Most of the Chinese, not different from Americans, are mostly looking inwards with 56 percent giving priorities to China's own problems. Only 22 percent of the Chinese support to help other countries to deal with their problems. That opinion does not quite match the 77 percent of Chinese who believe that their country plays a more important role in the world today compared to 10 years ago. They are right, but a rising importance in the global community goes hand in hand with the obligation to assume more responsibility.

The spotlight is on China, its achievements and goals and how it will execute its new role in the global community. In 2016 China could celebrate another milestone in its global positioning, as the Yuan became a component of the Special Drawing Right, the world's currency basket, understandably saluted by Chinese media. It is most likely that many have never heard of Special Drawing Right, which is no wonder as it is widely ignored outside the IMF. Nevertheless to the Chinese it was a confirmation of their status on the world stage as an economic and financial superpower.

China's armaments industry

China gains global influence by strategically extending its armaments industry. China has not only become strong enough to shake global stock markets, as it did in June 2015. By reaching the position as number three in market shares of conventional armaments exports, China also became a player in the industry (behind USA and Russia). Its exports rose 88 percent from 2011 to 2015. Its shares in global armaments export has grown to almost six percent and made it the world's third largest exporter. Nevertheless compared with a market share of 33 percent of US exports and 25 percent of Russia China is in its beginning. While its arms exports remain 75 percent in Asia, Turkey could become the first member of NATO to order weapons from China, if the export of missile defense systems to the country is signed (DIE ZEIT October 21, 2016).

The mood in the whole world is changing. Neither the global community nor the business world can afford to misinterpret China. If Chinese politics can guide China to leverage its full potential its position and importance will rise dramatically. But so does its responsibility as a member in the global community.

China's new role in global governance

China's engagement in global governance is part of the power shift in international systems. China's strategic position is very much determined on the judgment of China being at the center of an East–West axis in both continental and maritime territories. The importance of China's role in economic, security and legal fields of global policy making in international institutions is growing gradually. China's founding of the Asian Infrastructure Investment Bank underlines the country's determination to be in the center of reforms of global governance.

China's growing importance is evoking fear as well as exaggerated expectations on how it will contribute to the global community. Judgments will be made by what is done and not by what is said. This is true on the international as well as domestic stages.

But while the mindset of China's society will not change rapidly, individual rights play an increasingly larger role domestically and globally. How will China's position on individual rights and freedom cooperate with China's vision of global governance?

The Communist Party of China draws its legitimacy upon economic performance and loyalty from the achievements of the past.

People want to make money, and as long as the government provides an environment that allows improving their standard of living politics do not play a big role. But its growth in GDP has to be matched by a growth in household incomes.

The World Bank attributed China as an upper-middle income nation on its way to one of the world's advanced economies. That is also reflected in the mindsets of its people. The well-educated middle class is putting increasing weight on their voices to be heard. They do not question the system as such, but the execution of power in fields that affects them, such as implementation of the rule of law, environmental protection and better social safetynets.

But whatever flaws there are, Chinese do not want the West to give them lectures on how to move on and bring about change.

Chapter Four

Understanding the Emerging Players

Who Belongs to the Global Middle Class?

Many of the emerging economies, which we collectively call the Global Southern Belt, are about to play a much more important role in the global economy. There are of course huge differences in the level of development. It reaches from China, which is both a developed and an emerging economy, to countries that barely make it like Senegal, or worse, like Venezuela, which is not matching the criteria any more. We have left out Russia as it is dancing on the sidelines, emotionally leaning towards the West, strategically bonding with China and the Global Southern Belt, politically relevant but economically bumbling.

Even though there is a lot of reporting about the rise of a global middle class, we have to consider what middle class stands for. It is a subjective mindset as well as measurable objective criteria. It is of course as little homogeneous as are continents. And in judging needs and business opportunities we must differentiate between the various levels and cultural habits of the local middle class.

In the major shift of the world's economic balance, where does India stand? In 1994 India's official poverty ratio was 45 percent. According to 2017 Asian Development Data, 21.9 percent of India's population still lives below the national poverty line, and almost

18 percent of the employed population lives on less than $2 purchasing power per day. Around 600 million Indians are counted as middle class, even though largely in the lower middle class, spending between $4 and $10 per day. Looking at a global middle class one has to keep in mind that while the term is the same, conditions within the global middle class can be as big as the gap between rich and poor.

Global middle class stretches from $10 to $190 per day

According to the US *PewResearchCenter* from 2001 to 2011, worldwide, nearly 700 million people made it out of poverty, but the report says, most of them barely. In 2011, 16 percent of the world's population were living a little over the US poverty line, making a minimum $20 per day. Naturally poverty lines in developed countries differ greatly from those in emerging economies. By the definition of the *Brookings Institute* the US middle class starts at $41,000. The Department of Health and Human Services defines a US family of four living on $23,850 as poor. Switzerland considers a couple without children and an income around $70,000 as middle class. The Pew research center also found that 203 US metropolitan areas had a shrinking middle class. But decisive the point is that they were not slipping downwards, but moving up the leather into the wealthier families' category.

New markets, different purchasing power

The picture changes if we turn to Africa. According to an *Economist* study 90 percent of Africans are still earning less than $10 per day. The $10 to $20 middle class ($3650 to $7300 per year) is estimated at 6.2 percent. What is considered an upper middle class with a $20 to $25 income per day, has reached only 2.3 percent and would be considered very poor in the US and Europe. Large international companies such as Coca-Cola or Nestle had to admit that the growth of the African middle class is slow and does not repeat the much faster rise of the Asian middle class where relatively well-paid jobs in factories brought millions out of poverty. ASEAN countries are defining middle class with incomes ranging from $10 to $100 per day. Based on these numbers in 2012 almost 200 million people were counted as middle class. Nielson estimates the number to double by 2020 and reach 400 million. China, which barely had a middle class until the late 1990s, now has 225 million people with an income between $11,500 and $43,000 a year.

India's middle class, even if on the lower income level, is an important segment of its economy. Analyzing the changing demands and spending patterns is key to any economic decision and marketing policies. And just as it happened in China in the 1980s, those who want to get out of poverty are most likely to have the best chance in new and not yet well-organized sectors where they have to deal with fewer regulations. It is no surprise that almost one-third of India's lower middle class is seeking success as vendors, followed by those working in the food industry.

From an optimistic point of view a high potential lies in leveraging India's underused women workforce. Globally 40 percent of the workforce are women, in India, according to a 2017 World Bank report, only one-fourth of women are part of it. And according to estimates, with only 17 percent India's women have the lowest share in contributing of GDP, contributing 41 percent, in Sub Sahara Africa 39 percent and Latin America 33 percent. The World Bank estimates that if India would leverage the potential of women in the population the growth rate would rise above 9 percent. But sadly there is much more to correct in India's gender inequality than the percentage of working women.

Access to education plays a key role in social mobility. In rural India, still many parents have their children working in the fields rather than giving priority to their education. It is no surprise that globally, as well as in the two most populated countries, China and India, most of the new middle class is created in the cities. McKinsey estimates that by 2025 India will have 69 cities with more than one million people. Compared to China, where in the past 35 years almost 500 million people moved into cities, India's urban population rate is slower, but steady.

In both countries, urban infrastructure markets are booming, but China's urbanization is organized and systematically focusing on developing backwards and rundown areas. Without doubt it is India's cities that will be key in economic and social progress and in the transition to modernity. In its urbanization process India should be able to leverage its demographic advantage of a much larger young population.

In Asian, African and Latin American countries rapid urbanization and the rise of the middle class are interconnected. Communication and transportation industry, housing, food and health care, and especially in education the demand is rising in all lower and higher middle classes. But while consumption in African countries lags behind estimates the purchasing clout in Asian countries is rising.

In Latin America's countries middle class grew from 16 percent in 2001 to 27 percent in 2011. In addition, consumer behavior in Latin America, Africa and Asia are not the same. When we are in Latin America, *pura vida* (pure life) in almost all countries goes hand in hand with spending money for restaurants, hanging out with friends, having fun. Brazilians only save around 10 percent of their income while Chinese save almost one-third. Household savings in India now make less than a quarter of disposable income. While saving money plays a large role in all parts of China, the more south you go the more easy-going the life style will get. But everywhere in China wealth is rising.

Africa: From Foreign Aid to Myriads of Opportunities?

In India's emerging maritime strategy, the Indian Ocean, which connects and separates from the African continent, is gaining importance. East Africa is a key gateway to the Indian Ocean region which has large energy reserves and strategic waterways. India's relationships with East African nations, especially South Africa, Tanzania, Kenia and Mozambique are excellent. India–Africa Forum Summits aim to increase diplomatic relations and seize the economic opportunities. President Modi's 2016 first trip to African nations underscores that goal.

According to thehindu.com, India and Africa trade between March 2016 and 2017 reached $52 billion, exports to Africa reached $23 billion. Almost 8 percent of India's imports originate from African countries. Reason enough to take a closer look at the continent, whose picture in the world is still obsolete in many ways.

Whoever has been monitoring Africa has been an observer of an awakening. Unfortunately, just as it is the case with China, bad news about Africa finds its way into global media much faster than good news. Though bad news about North Sahara Africa will remain with us for a long time.

When we talk about Africa in this book we are concentrating on the Sub Saharan nations. Sad as it is we cannot expect too much progress of the Northern African states. Its population is deeply divided ethnically by Maghrebis, including Berbers, Copts, Egyptians and Fur, and religiously by the 14,000-year old conflict between the majority of Sunnis and the minority of Shiites. The Arab spring was much more uproar against economic misgovernment, corruption and inequality than a call for Western democracy, as it was embraced by the West. There was no history in nation building, no common ground to build on. The higher the barriers among them become the less likely are they can be torn down.

A compensation for frustration

Africa specialist Laurence Brahm, international lawyer, economist, author and founder of the Himalayan and African Consensus economic paradigms believes that "terrorism is not alone the result of fundamental religious beliefs as characterized in certain mainstream media. People turn to extreme measures when they have no outlet to vent their frustration over conditions of poverty, ethnic marginalization, or both. Often religious beliefs may tragically be used as a rationale or pretext for this extremism. Deep dissatisfaction followed by terrorism, are sequential reactions to the same sets of problems. The problems associated with the alienation of ethnic groups must be addressed at their root cause, through economic empowerment, education, healthcare, and returning to people what is theirs, recognition of their own individual diversity, identity and self-respect. Otherwise dissent and strife will not go away, regardless of how sophisticated the military technology and social re-engineering theories of constituent states."

Apart from the different stories of North and South Sahara Africa, Africa, just as Asia, is not a monolith. Its countries are as big as Algeria (2,381,741 sq km), which is 3.5 times the size of Texas, and as small as Gambia (10,120 sq km), which is less than twice the size of Delaware. Reaching almost $500 billion Nigeria has the largest GDP of all African nations, Sao Tome and Principe $333,000,000 GDP close the list with the smallest.

Africa's 54 sovereign states show multiple faces

One speaks of "Africa" as if it were a country; nevertheless each one of its 54 sovereign states shows various faces, from those shaken by conflicts, hopelessness and poverty to modern, vibrant, with a self-confident middle class.

One of its once most promising countries, South Africa, which in 2016 regained its position as Africa's largest economy, has lifted more than 3.5 million people out of extreme poverty in the past decade. And even though it is growing much slower than Asia's middle class, Africa's new middle class is the driving force in progress and its new 310 million-consumer class does not fit the old African cliché of a helpless, poor and lazy Africa any more. And yet, despite often high GDP growth, unemployment, poverty and inequality remain among the highest in the world. In addition Africa's economic outlook has darkened.

Nigeria, now back to being Africa's second largest economy, plummeted to a −13.70 percent in the first quarter of 2016 over the previous quarter with a high chance to slip into recession (Central Bank of Nigeria). All after a sensational jump to 33 percent GDP growth in 2004, and still reaching almost 7 percent in 2007. Young, dynamic microentrepreneurs and Nigeria's militant Islamist group Boko Haram show two diametrical sides of highly diverse mindsets, terror on one side, and entrepreneurship and ambition on the other.

Achieving sustainable goals

Despite all problems, according to August 2016 GSMA's Ecosystem accelerator, whose mission is to scale innovative and sustainable mobile services in emerging markets through partnerships between operators and innovators, the number of technology hubs in Africa has more than doubled from 117 in 2015 to 314 to August 2016. More than half of the hubs are located in only five countries, Egypt, Kenya, Nigeria, Morocco and South Africa, which leads the list with 54 hubs.

American investors and venture capitalists are increasingly investing in startups across the African continent. IBM launched innovation centers in Lagos and Casablanca. Large companies like Google and Microsoft established a $75 million 4 Africa project, considering that it is time to invest in Africa. In addition to its $12 million solar project investment in November 2015 Google announced to invest in Lake Turkana Wind Power Project, Africa's largest wind power farm in Kenya. The decline in bandwidth costs supports such investment and digital transformation is boosted across African countries. Solomon Assefa, IBM researcher and Vice President of Science and technology sees Africa transforming: "There is increased stability and lot of bandwidth that's come on line, tremendous economic growth, plus a lot of infrastructure being built and a lot of foreign investment."

One of Africa's largest problems is the lack of infrastructure, lack of roads and lack of a banking system, which led to a booming e-commerce. But paying for product online was not an easy task as the advance of the telecommunication systems were slow and waiting times for landlines long. With the launch of PayPal in 2014 Nigeria became the world's third largest mobile e-commerce market with transactions of more than $610 million in 2015, and PayPal estimates to hit $819 million in 2016. While these numbers are mostly international transactions e-commerce also holds great opportunities for small and local merchants targeting the new middle class. Kenya's M-Pesa is one of Africa's still relatively few success stories in mobile financial services that offer a lower cost, easier accessible alternative to traditional banking. Especially as already two-thirds of Sub Saharan adults are using mobile phones.

At the 2016 Samsung Africa Forum held in February in Monaco, Samsung Electronic presented "Innovations that transform people's lives". The Samsung Electronic Africa company also announced "that it will bolster its Corporate Citizenship efforts in Africa in a bid to help the continent achieve sustainable developing goals". Samsung is engaged to use its digital technology to transform learning processes in African countries. Solar powered Internet Schools, Smart Schools and E-Learning Academies can provide solutions to improve learning by transforming the teaching and learning processes. It will help to reduce the number of school dropouts and graduates to enter the job market successfully.

New openings for average Africans

New ideas are changing not only consumer habits but opening opportunities for average Africans without the need of large investments.

Airbnb is not only changing tourist behavior, it also generates income for people who are willing to rent their places. In South Africa alone more than 130,000 guests stayed in an Airbnb accommodation in 2015. Cape Town leads with 10,000 listings followed by Johannesburg with 2000, creating an average income for the hosts of $2260 per year. Samantha Allenberg, Uber's communications associate for Africa refers to Uber's social impact: "We have enabled thousands of work opportunities across Africa and believe we can enable thousands more in the coming years." Uber has established a presence in eight African cities and believes in a high potential for growth given the rising middle class.

Investments tailored to the specifics of African countries

Africans do not just wait and see what international companies can offer. Local entrepreneurs are developing African-tailored digital products. Examples are Ruanda's support of tourism and coffee plants, Kenya's IT experts and mobile phone apps, and Ethiopia's flower exports. Botswana is dedicated to retrieve the value added chain for diamonds into the country. In the future it will not only export raw diamonds, but also process the stones in country.

The vast majority of Africa's middle class consumers are operating in digital space. Frost & Sullivan estimates that Internet penetration will reach 75 percent by 2020. The number of mobile phones in Africa has reached 650 million. To young Africans who are increasingly online and benefitting from rising access to information, it has become the door opener to create their own businesses. It also supports civil society and speeds up social change.

Under the headline "Artists thrive in Africa as freedom grows," the *New York Times* wrote about the positive impact "the growth of democratic expectations, the decline of dictatorships and the explosion of the Internet" have on the flourishing of African artists. Step by step new projects and products are creating a colorful art scene: Nigerian's film industry, known as Nollywood, the Rift valley Festival in Kenya, and literary journals like *Kwani?*, the flagship publication founded by some of Kenya's most exciting new writers.

Africa's art scene is increasingly detaching from European American influence striving for more self-sufficiency. "In Africa," writes Ginanne Brownell in the *New York Times* in January 2013, "even in the world of art, the road to financial support and recognition has long passed through the West. But the ever shifting landscape of African politics and economics and a protracted financial crisis in the West have led a growing network of artists, curators and nonprofit organizations to seek ways of detaching the continent's art world from its Euro American axis."

Africa will remain one of the fastest growing regions

The latest data published by World Bank's new *Africa's Pulse,* analyzes economic trends and data on the African continent. Its 2014 overall outlook is that Sub Sahara, due to substantial investment in infrastructure, is experiencing a strong recovery in agriculture, expansion of services, electricity capacity and transport. Africa will remain one of the fastest growing regions with economic growth rising from 4.6 percent in 2014 to 5.2 percent in 2015–2016.

The question whether the continent will manage to change into a bright future remains open. Our judgment is based equally on counting on Africa's potential as it is on what can actually be seen today on the ground today. And so do investors. In a study that analyzed 44 Sub Saharan nations the Bill & Melinda Gates Foundation calculates the potential of digitalization holds for African countries. Based on the level of digitalization rate in Kenya unleveraged possible enhancement reaches from 28 percent in South Africa to 155 percent in Ethiopia. A large part of the mobile providers' market is unexploited, but better understanding needs more and more reliable data.

The arguments for "myriads of opportunity" are based on the mindset of Africa's young population who does not carry the heavy baggage of colonial victim mentality. Poor governing in many African countries discourages and limits the engagement of young entrepreneurs. One of the pillars supporting Africa's growth is as we said before, China, which is also Africa's largest trading partner. China's century infrastructure project, the new maritime Silk Road, holds great opportunities to give African countries and industries better access to trade streams and global markets.

All in all we would not go as far as former President of Nigeria, Olusegun Obansanjo, who predicted the 21st century to be Africa's century, and maybe not as far as Berger's myriads of opportunities. But we are optimistic. What is needed is entrepreneurial spirit, guts, innovative ideas, and rewards for good efforts.

India–Africa relations

While China remains the largest investor in Africa, India has been well aware of Africa's potential. Already in 2002 India launched its "Focus Africa" program to strengthen and revitalize its ties to the continent. Since 2008 India–Africa Forum Summits and the Africa Forum Summit, held in New Delhi in October 2015 are supporting trade and investment relations.

South Africa remains the leading export destination for Indian products, followed by Kenya, Egypt, Tanzania and Nigeria. India has also undertaken investment initiatives making it one of the largest investors in Africa. Indian's automobile industry, telecommunication and construction companies are among them, participating in energy, IT services, power and infrastructure. With 52 percent, the largest imports from Africa to India are petroleum products.

Bilateral trade between India and Africa has increased from $1billion in 1995 to $75 billion in 2015.

India and Africa share the common history of colonization and it claims that its model of development should differ from other countries and be built on mutual beneficiary and partnerships. One of the contributions is the extension of scholarships to African students and the Indian Technical and Economic Cooperation program with the goal to build and support human capital and institutional capacity.

And Europe's African politics?

On November 12, 2015, the EU and 24 African countries proudly announced the so-called Valetta Action Plan. Clear definition of interests and demands could signal a turn, if not a change of paradigms, as Germany's foreign ministry formulated. The EU founded a trust in which 1.8 billion Euro was paid from its own household. Each of the 28 members was asked to add on a voluntary base. But up to date, October 2016, only 81 million were added.

"Africa can only save itself," was the basic line of Paul Collier, Professor at Oxford University and adviser to the German Finance

Ministry as Germany is taking over the presidency of the G20 in 2017. Africa's migration to him adds to the problem of brain drain as mostly the most active and most creative are leaving. Collier sees the main problem in lecturing local governments what to do and in too much concentration on social matters. "If we take away the responsibility of African governments to provide housing and schools for their people how can the people give them the back-up needed to advance their countries."

In his opinion the key are enterprises though not much liked by aid agencies. "But", he says, "enterprises bring wealth. They are a motor of progress and can trigger comprehensive social change. That exactly what happened in China."

Taking destiny in their own hands

By our own experience we know that presenting China as a model does not play well in the West. It is a good sign that Collier underscores "when I was a child, China was dirt poor, today it is an economic powerhouse. If everything goes well, a country needs one generation to overcome poverty."

"Great Britain has fought a war with China to swamp the country with opium. The Chinese did not get discouraged. I do not want to belittle colonialism in Africa, but if we declare Africans victims we are incapacitating them. In my experience, especially young Africans do not want to hear that any more. There is a generation, which wants to take destiny in their own hands. Those people are the future."

Asia: From Learning from the West to the World's Dominating Continent

Asia is outstanding in many ways. It is the most populated continent with China the most populated country. Russia is the largest country in the world. The Himalayas are the world's highest mountain chain, Baikal is the deepest and oldest inland lake in the world, Mariana is the deepest part of the world's oceans and the Dead Sea has the lowest elevation on land and the saltiest body of water. India is known as the world's largest democracy.

Asia has the most intercontinental countries and countries reaching into another continent; among these countries are Russia, Kazakhstan, Indonesia, Japan, Egypt, and Turkey. Asia plays an important role as the cradle of many cultures. Most world religions originated in Asia.

Asia is special to us for it was *Megatrends Asia* that brought us together as author and publisher. At that time we did not know that our later life as a couple and as coauthors would be tightly connected to Asia and China. Although when *Megatrends Asia* was written in 1994 it was clear to us that Asia would play a major role in the coming decades: "What is happening in Asia is by far the most important development in the world today. Nothing else comes close, not only for Asians but for the entire planet. The modernization of Asia will forever reshape the world as we move towards the next millennium."

The book ended: "During the last 150 years of progress and prosperity enjoyed in the West, much of Asia was in poverty. Now Asians are on their way into a Renaissance, and opportunity for them to reassert the grandeur and glory of their civilizations. Combined with science and technology, Asians could provide the world with a new model. One that takes modernization and combines it with the virtues of Eastern and Western values by reconciling freedom and order, individualism and communitarian concerns. The most profound consequence of the rise of the East is the birth of a new model for modernization."

Asian countries are opportunity-oriented. At first the "Four Tigers," Hong Kong, Singapore, South Korea and Taiwan achieved strong growth and rapid industrialization between 1960 and 1990. Singapore leapfrogged over the industrial stage to push full force into the information age. The city-state developed the world's most sophisticated infrastructure and became an operational center for multinational firms. Hong Kong rose to the fiercest competitor in global finance to London and New York. South Korea became world leader in manufacturing high-tech quality products.

China's people liberation army as innovator

One of the most surprising frontrunners in entrepreneurial inventiveness was China's People Liberation Army (PLA). Facing painful cuts in their budget, they did not seek the solution by cutting down, but by seeking opportunities to make money. Not much in the media limelight between 1984 and 1995 the PLA set up more than 20,000 companies with profits of about $5 billion, which made it the largest and most profitable commercial empire in China. It was estimated that half of China's military personnel were engaged in non-military commercial activities.

ASEAN: 70 Million households in the consuming class

A little after *Megatrends Asia* was published the 1997 Asian Financial crisis shocked the markets and led to many voices writing Asia off. Way too quickly, as we know. East Asia was replacing Japan as the driver of the region's booming economy. In 1995, Japan's GDP was in the fifth consecutive year of stagnation. The prediction of *Megatrends Asia* that Japan was on a long downward slide has sadly been proven true.

Despite Japan's stagnation Asia's growing importance in the global economy will continue boost some of the world's fastest growing countries, among them now India, an increasingly stronger Korea and the fast growing Association of South East Asian Nations (ASEAN).ASEAN was formed almost 50 years ago, and remained without a great presence on the world stage for some time. Over the years their 10 members gained increasing importance: Indonesia, Malaysia, the Philippines, Singapore, Thailand, Brunei, Myanmar, Cambodia, Laos and Vietnam. With now 600 million people and a combined GDP of $2.4 trillion (2014), ASEAN countries have become an economic powerhouse among the countries of the Global Southern Belt. If it were a single country, its GDP would rank as seventh largest in the world. It is the fourth largest exporting region in the world behind the EU, North America and China.

Oxford Economics estimates Asia's share in the global economy near 45 percent by 2025. Asia does not only cover about one-third of the landmass of the globe, it is also on the path to be the dominant continent as the by far fastest growing region of the world. Asia stands out in many regards.

A changing landscape in the corporate world

In its Special Report on Business in Asia, May 31, 2014, the *Economist* wrote: "By 2030 Asia will have surpassed North America and Europe combined in terms of global power, based upon GDP, population size, military spending and technological investment." Some of the world's giant companies are in Asia: PetroChina $203 billion; ICBC, China, $198 billion; Samsung Electronics, Korea $161 billion; Toyota, Japan $193 billion; China Construction Bank $162 billion; Alibaba, China $200 billion; tsmc, Taiwan $101 billion, to just mention the companies joining the $100 plus billion club. To compare: India's largest enterprise is Reliance Industries $50.6 billion (*Forbes* data and *The Economist*).

In comparison: Apple $586 billion, Siemens, Germany, $91 Billion, Novartis, Switzerland, $203 billion.

The top 10 in the *Forbes* list is half US, half China. The five Chinese companies are state owned, the five US companies are private. But as part of President Xi's rejuvenation of China, China's state-owned enterprises need to open up to private investment as well.

Asia now accounts for 27 percent of the world's market capitalism; Asia's consumer market is huge, 30 percent of the world's middle class spending; 47 percent of the world's manufacturing takes place in Asia. Almost 55 percent of Asia's trade is within the region.

This is the context of the continent in which China's started its One Belt One Road initiative, the revival of the maritime and landline Silk Road. There is no question it will be part of the economic transformation of the next decades with impact on all other continents. We will deal with more details in Chapter Five, A New Mapping of the World.

Latin America: One and a Half Steps Forward and One Step Back

Would half of the drive and the rhythm Latin American people have in their blood be implemented in their economy it would be global success story. Maybe it is the beautiful landscapes and the sunshine that leads to the general underlying positive spirit of its people despite all obvious problems. And whether it is the Carnival of Rio, the taste Caipirinha on a bar at the shore, the tango and its *pura vida* lifestyle, Latin America has the bonus of the sympathy of the world.

On the ground, if you get closer to know Latin American countries and the people, the sunny picture shows the shades of the clouds. Administrations, judicial systems, public safety, courts and the parliaments are often weak points in the system. Though the positive side of the weakness of public services is that Latin Americans developed a strong sense of self-responsibility. They simply do not wait for the state to jump in when they are able to take life in their own hands.

Thanks to the happy nature of its people the countries of Latin America stumbled into globalization without having a clear picture of their role in it. And they neglected a key pillar of global trade: good infrastructure. That lack became the opportunity of the now biggest investor in Latin American infrastructure projects, China. It has invested more in Latin America's domestic infrastructure than in any other region, even though it China's share of the regions total FDI is still only 6 percent. In the overall picture Latin America and China are moving closer together while America and Latin America are drifting further apart. China–Latin America trade rose quickly from 2 percent in the year 2000 to 11 percent in 2010. America's once strong influence is declining.

Whether the US is unwilling or unable to compete with China's engagement in Latin America, the result remains the same. Very different from the USmarket-driven strategies, the Chinese approach their goals with a strategy developed over thousands of years: "practice strategic thinking." Master Sun already in his piece "The Art of War," dating back to the 5th century BC, was encouraging the

Chinese to develop a coordinated panoramic view which in our days is applied in China's approach to geopolitics.

Latin America has benefitted from the massive Chinese investment and so did the USA. And it is not the Chinese, but the free markets which allowed Huawei to surpass Ericsson, now building many of Latin America's telecommunication networks, in Brazil for example six out of seven 4G mobile phone networks. But benefitting from a growing consumer market it is not limited to mobile phone networks. French multinational retailer Carrefour achieved a 9.7 percent rise in its Latin American sales (currency effects included), and a 25 percent rise in Brazil.

To counterbalance an overdependence on China Latin American countries are keen to boost trade with India

India's exports to Mexico reached $2.8 billion in 2015–2016. During the same period, exports to Brazil, once India top export destination in LA countries, fell more than 50 percent from $5.9 billion in 2014–2015 to $2.6 billion.

But despite all of Latin America's current political and economic struggle, it would be a mistake to underestimate the potential of the market in the longer run. The Indian government promotes its exports to Asian and African countries. It will be smart to extend larger lines of credit to LAC countries to increase its share of Latin America's foreign trade.

The bed is made for investments

Today's Latin America and the 33 Caribbean countries make up one of the world's most diverse regions. Their population has grown to 642 million. But for millennia the population was not more than about 30 million people. It has a rich history in which many of its indigenous cultures, some highly civilized like the Aztec, Inca and Maya, developed independently of other world cultures. Their cultural development was brutally interrupted in 1492, when Christopher

Columbus, the Italian born explorer, set foot on the "New World" under the flag of the Spanish King Ferdinand. At the turn of the 16th century, Pedro Alvarez Cabral, the Portuguese navigator and explorer led a fleet of Portuguese ships and claimed the new territory now known as Brazil for the Portuguese King Manuel I. It was the Latin origin of the languages of the conquerors, Spanish and Portuguese, which gave "Latin America" its name.

After rough political and economic times in the 20th century, Latin American countries are mostly democratic and mostly market-driven economies. In the north, Venezuela's, Bolivia's and Ecuador's extreme socialism has resulted in the countries slip to the bottom of the 2016 *Heritage Foundation* Economic Freedom Ranking, positioned 175 and 158 and 159 in the category repressed. According to Inter-American Dialogue, from 2007 to 2016, China State Banks loaned $60 billion to Venezuela. But given Nicolas Madura's negative records of mismanaging the country's economy, China and Chinese companies are running out of patience. According to the American Enterprise Institute (AEI) since 2010 Chinese companies have invested around $2.5 Billion each year, according to in the first half of 2016 the amount only reached $300.

On the Western side of the continent the Pacific Alliance (PA) with its members Chile, Colombia, Costa Rica, Mexico, Peru and Panama take a market-oriented approach with the goal to improve transparency and efficiency in capital flows, goods, rule of law and the protection of intellectual property. In May 2008 the Union of South American Nations, now signed by all 12 independent South American countries, was founded. Its goal is economic integration and a common currency, parliament and passports. American commentators interpreted this move as a pivotal development in the loss of the United States hegemony in the region.

Pacific Alliance versus Bolivian Alliance

It is no surprise to us that PA nations have attracted far more direct foreign investment in the past decade than ALBA (data Heritage Foundation, World Bank).

Latin America is also contributing to the global middle class, reaching a watershed in 2011 when for the first time its middle class outnumbered people living in poverty. Alongside China and Eastern Europe it is one of the three regions with the greatest middle class expansion between 2001 and 2011 (defined by the Pew Institute earning $10 to $20 per day), and now accounts for 30 percent of the population (World Bank 2014). The continent is on a new and better path. In the competition for growth Paraguay leads: World Bank estimates a growth rate of 11 percent, followed by Panama 9 percent and Peru with 6 percent.

Latin Americans are hungry for education, hungry for success and ready to grab the opportunities offered by the transformation of the coming decades. As our friend and former Latin American correspondent Dr. Wolfgang Stock, who just returned from a trip to Peru, said: "The bed is made, and Latin American governments are able to turn weaknesses into strength. Direct Foreign investment is not only about building infrastructure, it is also about creating jobs and new markets for both the investor and the local regions."

Our friend Walter Link, adviser to Brazilian enterprises and CEOs, sees the difficulty in the political and business establishment who wants to keep the *status quo* while opposition and young entrepreneurs want to achieve real change. It seems that the fact that quite a number of CEOs have not only been investigated but also sentenced to many years in jail is a clear sign to move from lip service to action.

Reforms are partly sluggish, but sincere efforts are made. Sustainable progress will not come unless natural rich countries in Latin America will depend less on their natural recourses and long-term planning is tightly connected. Any major investment takes time to show results. But political thinking does not operate in long-term thinking but in election-driven considerations. How to escape that circle is not only a miracle question for Latin America and the Caribbean, but also for Western democracies as such. But what is true for Africa is true for Latin America, their countries have to find the solution by themselves. No one can do it for them.

Chapter Five

A New Mapping of the World

To Master the Future, We have to Understand the Past

This book is not written for just one country or audience. It is addressed to people in various continents. Therefore, we can assume that its readers will look at the world in different ways. And even what we described will not be received in the same way. Most people look at the globe with their own country in the center of interest, maybe picturing their country to be the center. The environment in which we grew up, our family, our culture our country shaped the worldview we have now. But as with almost everything, from time to time thoughts and things need an examination and an update. More so if how it was shaped goes way back to the past.

The long tail of the past

Hegemonies, powerful sovereigns and leading intellectuals in all continents created spheres of influence within and beyond their borders. The Vedas, a simple pretheism, in India, which are estimated to have been written as early as 1500–100 BC, are likely to be the oldest religious writings in the world. Think of Socrates, Plato and Aristotle and the foundation of philosophy, Athens as the cradle of democracy, the Iliad and Odyssey and the art of poetry. Athens's and Rome's political, legal and cultural influences are still with us today. The German Book of Civil Law (Buergerliches Gesetzbuch) until today is based on jurisprudence of the 19th century, which goes back to Roman law. The Roman Empire in Europe, The Kingdom of Kush and the Egyptians in Africa, the Five Hegemons and the Zhou Dynasty in China, the cultures of the Inca, Maya and Aztecs in South America all left their footprints on global culture.

A Tale of 2000 Years

Thanks to the American Economist Angus Madison (1926–2010), we can get an estimate about the economic development of the past more than 2000 years. Some will say it's gimmick, others take it seriously, but it is the best approximation there is given the lack of data, the shift in borders and other obstacles that work against accurate numbers over the centuries. Even though his calculations are not without controversy, it puts things in perspective.

As history shows the history of the US as the most powerful military might and as the dominating economy is significant, as it is short. Some ranks are surprising, such as Italy's position around the 15th and 16th centuries. Even at the time of Jesus's birth, when the Roman Empire was a world power and Italy its center, the country only made it to rank third.

During the first 1,000 years of Madison's calculation, India was the leading nation. Looking at the picture 500 years later, in 1500, the powers of the West were still behind India and the new leader, China. And India would only be able to gain the top of the list one more time in 1700. The year, which would turn out to be the only year between 1500 and 2015 in which neither the United States nor China led the world.

In 1820, when the industrial revolution began to show impact, the United Kingdom finally appeared on the economic leadership map.

In the light of this timeframe it is not a surprise that China is by far not a newcomer on top of the GDP hierarchy, but simply reasserting the leading position it had lost in the late 19th century to the United States.

Year

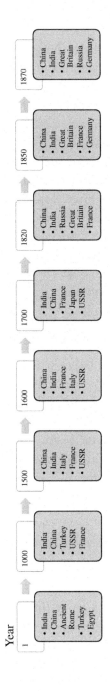

| 1 | 1000 | 1500 | 1600 | 1700 | 1820 | 1850 | 1870 |

1
- India
- China
- Ancient Rome
- Turkey
- Egypt

1000
- India
- China
- Turkey
- USSR
- France

1500
- China
- India
- Italy
- France
- USSR

1600
- China
- India
- France
- Italy
- USSR

1700
- India
- China
- France
- Japan
- USSR

1820
- China
- India
- Russia
- Great Britain
- France

1850
- China
- India
- Great Britain
- France
- Germany

1870
- China
- India
- Great Britain
- Russia
- Germany

In addition to the 2000-year overview Maddison established in 2001, Madison estimated the economic output the global economy achieved in the years of one to have been $105.4 billion, measured on the price basis of the year 1990. It was less than the economic power of Berlin in February 2016, which reached 124.6 billion Euros. (To avoid currency fluctuations and various price levels in different countries Maddison's calculations were on the basis of GDP Purchasing power parity).

In 1500, the largest city in the world was Beijing, with an estimated population of 600,000 to 700,000 people. With a GDP of estimated $100 billion, China was the largest economy in world, followed closely by India. France ranked third with a GDP of approximately $18 million and Paris as the largest city in Europe with 200,000 people. Rome, once the center of the Roman Empire, had declined to irrelevance with the Pope moving to Avignon. (The Maddison-Project, 2013 version.)

The year 1517, a turning point in Europe's history

It was the European Renaissance, with its beginnings in the 14th century in Italy, which had started to undermine Christian dogma by scientific findings heralding the shift from the dominating theocentric (God in the center) worldview to a much more anthropocentric (mankind in the center) worldview. When Humanism as an education movement merged with critical opinions about the theological foundation of Catholicism, the shedding of the power of the hegemon gained momentum.

The shedding of the power of the hegemon

About a decade before Babur established the Mughal Empire, in the year 1517, the Catholic monk Martin Luther nailed a memorandum of protest on the porch of the Church of Wittenberg Castle. One man's act that would turn into an avalanche soon to sweep away old worldviews and to shake the foundation of the most powerful force of the time: the Catholic Church. It was a turning point in history, over time the game changer for the most powerful institution in Europe, the Catholic Church. The Church's power reached into worldly power of kings, emperors, dukes and its dogma held science hostage.

The powerful cultural and education movement had spread from Northern Italy to most of Europe. Transition started with questions and doubts, a search for alternatives, a shift in mindsets and different views to once accepted positions. Education supported the interplay of cultural, social, political factors and opened the minds of the people. Paired with a rapid urbanization it created the opportunity to reach modest wealth for people of various professions and made cities prosperous. Education in the hands of the Church and its economic strength had been strong pillars of the hegemony of the Catholic Church. With the spreading of the Renaissance and Reformation access to education made its way down the social ladder.

With the crumbling of its power the geocentric worldview had to give way to the heliocentric worldview and science began to shake off the shackles of religious limitations that had held it hostage for more than a millennium. The decline of the power of the Catholic Church gained momentum. But the end of its hegemony would not have been possible without the fundamental changes of the time.

The root of Europe's real hegemon

The rise of the Catholic Church began 1700 years ago, when the Roman heir to the throne, Constantine, became the ruler of the Roman Empire. Constantine was the first Roman Emperor to be baptized as a Christian. It was a U-turn from Roman polytheisms to Christian monotheism. And it allowed Constantine to underscore his authorization by a parallel: God was the sole ruler in heaven, and Constantine was the sole God-blessed Roman Emperor on earth.

It was the beginning of collaboration of the Catholic Church (the only recognized religion) and the State. Tightly interconnected, each supported the power of the other to achieve mutual benefits. Inequality was God-given. Clergy, nobility, citizen, farmer was the social hierarchy. Each rank had its place; each rank had its courts.

In those days epidemics and plagues caused high mortality, and people without worldly prospect were longing for salvation in after-life. The only place to turn to was the Church. But over time segments of the Catholic Church had degenerated from serving believers to capitalizing on the needs of believers. The door to heaven had a price tag, until in the 15th century when things began to change.

In the meanwhile, by 1890, on the other side of the Atlantic Ocean, the US finally emerged as the world's largest economy, still followed by China, the United Kingdom and Japan, while Europe, which was split into countries and dukedoms, could not compete in the size of GDP to make it into Maddison's list.

The beginning of a Westerncentric world

During the following 500 years, but especially in the past 100 years, none of the global cultures gained such comprehensive global influence as did Europe and later the United States of America, which, after all, and beside the slowly exterminated native Indians, was at first mostly populated by European immigrants. Their political, economic and cultural influence spread to the world, overwhelming local cultures in most continents. Western clothing, Western music, Western business practices, inventions and innovations spread from the West to the rest of the world. Over time this led to a Western self-perception of superiority over other parts of the world. The West saw itself as the moral authority to set global standards based on a Westerncentric worldview, judging the world by and against Western standards.

The crumbling of Western authority and power

As we travel the world and do our research, we see the global authority of the West is no longer unchallenged, and the Western worldview no longer accepted as universal. Emerging economies around the globe are developing their own standards. In fact the term "emerging economies" as such has somewhat outlived itself. It has lost its usefulness in updating the picture of the global community. Depending on the focus, some countries, such as China, are both developed and underdeveloped. Qatar, which has the highest per capita GDP, still counts as an emerging economy.

The tale of two countries begins

In the initial decades of the 20th century, the leadership of the United States became more and more obvious. Nevertheless, in 1930 China although shaken by social disorder and divided between nationalists and communists, and encroached by the Japanese, was still the second largest economy though only one-third of the size of the US with little difference to Germany, the UK and India.

The turning point for the China in reasserting its leading position

By 1980, 50 years and two World Wars later, Japan had conquered the second place, Germany third. China had slipped to number 10 beaten by India ranking number nine. But with Deng Xiaoping's reform and opening up it became time for China to move up the GDP hierarchy again.

By 2015 the IMF projections showed China to have recovered to ranking first by GDP–PPP (purchasing power parity). Ranking number one by GDP is just a matter of time. Price Waterhouse Coopers (PWC) sees even more significant changes in the decades to come. By 2050 PWC expects China to have a GDP of $61 trillion, India regaining its second place with $ 42 trillion, tightly beating the US with $41 trillion. It seems the historical powers of the past and the relative newcomer on the global stage will dominate the future. But the best position on the rostrum is not in question. The Middle Kingdom will regain the laurels of the largest. Of greater importance for people might still be the competition of the laurels of the best country to live in.

While we are not willing to venture out into a distance with its billions and trillions of decisions, unforeseeable developments and startling surprises the safest bet is on China's leading role. If, in a simple calculation, we take the random distribution of talent and connect it with the population, China and India as the most populated countries could rise to enormous heights.

But countries do not develop following any theory of probability. The safest way to anticipate the future was and is to study the present.

From a Westerncentric to a Multicentric World

The nations of the Global Southern Belt will create a new mapping of the world. While the nations of the Global Southern Belt are in different stages of their development and growth, and a number of them in economic and political turbulence, they will collectively create a new mapping of the world.

Western hegemony has been diminished from various directions. Reduced by a gradual loss of economic power, its claim to own the global growth formula of democracy and free markets is no longer sustainable. New dynamics are transforming the global community. The Westerncentric world is fading into a multicentered world in which many countries and even more important, "a world of cities" will set the tone in global matters. It is a great opening up to a mix of opinions, economic and cultural diversity and, in a longer timeframe, new governing models. The game changers will be the countries and cities of the Global Southern Belt, which will reshape our world in the decades to come.

Why bother at all with the past when we have to master the future?

As we wrote in Chapter One, we do not start our lives as blank sheets. How we see the world and our country's position in it is very much dependent on the domestic and personal environments. And just as our thinking is highly influenced by the atmosphere of our upbringing, a country's self-perception is also shaped by its past.

Improvements are not limited to the West. If we look back more than 200 years inequality was mostly within countries dividing land-owning aristocrats and commoners into have and have-nots. Social mobility was very low and poor conditions often accepted as god-given destiny. Two hundred years later the large-scale gap was between developed and underdeveloped countries.

A new mapping of the world is not only about economics and politics; it is also about emotions and how to deal with them. During the 200-year dominance of the West the self-perception of the West as the dominant power and moral authority has strengthened. And we have to admit that the West has not only reached high GDPs but also high per capita income and a high quality of living, even though inequality within Western countries has become an increasing burden and party-political argument. Now that the position of the West is increasingly questioned by emerging economies and by its own shortcomings, both sides, the nations of the West, and the nations of the Global Southern Belt, have to rearrange in a new evolving world order.

Will the Global Structures of the Past be Able to Master the Future?

The structure of the UN and Bretton Woods institutions largely represent global power 70 years ago. Neither global institutions nor Western governments will be able to continue wielding the baton over an orchestra of emerging economies. Global governance organizations, launched by the West for the benefit of the West, have dominated the political scene since the end of the Second World War. But the world is not the same as when the UN, IMF, the World Bank were founded.

"I argue that while these institutions may have had some success in dealing with the 20th century problems, they have not been able to adapt to new global challenges that face us today," writes Ian Goldin, former Vice President of the World Bank in his book *Divided Nations, Why Global Governance is Failing and What We Can Do About It.*

The UN was created in 1945 as the successor of the League of Nations. Its goal was to foster peace and create a forum for friendly negotiations between states. Besides structural problems in the organization, sprawled mandates, donor interests, low employment turnover and therefore rapidly aging skills make it difficult to deal with existing problems let alone future issues.

The UN is far away from implementing the words of the bible written on the statue of the government of the USSR, donated in 1959 to the UN headquarter in New York: "Let Us Beat Our Swords Into Ploughshares."

The World Bank, founded at the 1944 Bretton Woods conference, was originally meant to rebuild Europe but found its core mission in providing capital for emerging economies. The World Banks's directive to alleviate poverty often resulted in the demand of "structural adjustments," with government cutbacks, leading to often catastrophic conditions for the developing countries.

The IMF core goal is exchange rate stability, although its mandates have mushroomed to include everything from financial regulation to the promotion of clean air.

Mastering global governance in the 21st century

The evolving new world order has heavy implications on the demands of global governments. Within the next decades the individual megatrends will lead to a systemic, integrated change, a global transformation, politically, economically, socially and procedurally. Consequently the complexity of increasing interdependence in all these processes has led to an advent of new systemic risks and it exposed the alarming shortcomings of global institutions.

An example of these shortcomings was the 2008 financial crisis. Global institutions were not able to prevent or effectively respond to the crisis. And yet the obvious failure has not led to triggered structural changes. The current structures of global institutions are not directed to address multiple systemic risk of the 21st century. While on one hand global institutions are in higher need than ever, their capacity to reform and innovate does not hold up with the speed of innovation and the growth of risks.

According to the IMF and WTO global foreign investment inflow increased 18 times between 1980 and 2005. Real global GDP rose by an estimated 32 percent and world merchandise imports and exports increased more than seven times. Global migration, hardly addressed by global institutions, in 2015 reached 244 million international migrants, the highest number ever recorded. The European Union received more than 1.2 million first time asylum claims in 2015. Despite the large number, put in perspective with the total EU population of almost 510 million, adequate refugee management should have been able to be dealt with.

There is a lot of lip service to the necessity of adapting global institutions to the complexity and interconnectedness and interdependencies of the 21st century. Global systemic risks affecting domestic policies pass over geopolitical and national interests and raise the need for intergovernmental negotiations.

How fast structural change in global institutions can be achieved is largely connected to the acceptance of the reality of new global power balances.

To let go of the past is a precondition to embrace the future

Albert Einstein's words, "I have to give up who I am to become who I have the potential to be," have not lost their relevance.

The degree to which we as people are mastering megatrends is highly linked to the degree to which we master ourselves. How much are we able to let go of obsolete opinions and take the challenge of developing new mindsets matching current conditions? What is true for each person is true on larger scales. How often do we hear about people and institutions holding on to habits and even more so, accrued rights, even if they harm the system as a whole.

The times as guardian of universal values are over

It does not serve the West and it will not change the overall direction if the West holds on to celebrating itself as the guardian of universal values and rights, defending its status as ethic and economic hub of the global community.

The emerging markets of the Global Southern Belt, for some time underestimated by the West, have gradually developed their own worldview. Based on their own history and culture they are laying a new ground based on their outlook for the future instead of running by the burdens of the past. They have discovered that instead of being directed by the West they could as well support each other. And they discovered that they were able to stand on their own feet. The proclaimed "End of History" turned into the "Global Game Change" for new economic alliances in the context of changing worldviews, new geopolitical weighting and new economic arrangements.

A New Group Dynamic in the Global Community

On first sight China, Africa, and Latin America have little in common. The easygoing Latin American lifestyle has yet to find its way to cope with often ambitious Chinese working ethics. In Africa tribes each with its own cultures are living in 58 countries making it difficult to build on common ground.

The Chinese population is rather homogeneous while Latin America's 20 countries are made up of a confluence of origins, reaching from the minority of native South Americans to French, Spanish and Portuguese, and also German immigrants. But as ethnically diverse as the cultures, as different as their histories, China, Africa and Latin America are bonding, bringing new dynamics to the global community. China is the leader in bringing hundreds of millions out of poverty. Latin America's advances in reducing poverty, despite great problems, have been remarkable over the last one and a half decades.

A World Bank Africa Poverty Report shows the paradox that while poverty may be lower than estimated, the number of people living in extreme poverty has risen. One of the reasons is a high fertility rate. On average, women in Sub-Sahara give birth to five children, the global average is 2.5 children.

China's own rise, its economic power, its politics of long-term strategic planning and its ability to implement reforms has created a platform for Latin American and African countries to collaborate in their shared goals of economic growth, social stability and progress. The dynamics of the Chinese engagements opens many possibilities for advancing win–win relationships among emerging economies. Improvements in the rule of law should enforce their multilateral relationships and support moving into the next stage from commerce to investment.

As the Atlantic Council reports in 2015, since the year 2000, trade among China and Latin America has grown nearly 2000 percent, supported by free trade agreements mainly with countries such as Chile and Peru. The decline of the commodity boom has been weakening this pillar. China wants to diversify its markets and commodity sources, and its investments.

Latin American countries want to loosen their ties to their main trading partners the US and Europe without turning themselves into the hands of China. By 2016 China became the second largest source of Latin American imports (US holds number one) and the third largest destination for its exports. According to statistics of National Statistic institutes, Central Banks and IMF, Brazil became China's main Latin American partner with a trade flow of about $78 billion in 2014. Good news for Brazil, which is dealing with recession and political scandals. China has also announced its intention to increase its investment in Latin America in $250 billion and trade flow to $500 billion by 2016.

Building on the past

China's rising influence in Asian and African countries is often seen as a development of the 20th and 21st centuries even though China's naval history goes way back to pre-Christian times. Its relations with Asian and African countries over the centuries are covered poorly in teaching history and in fact are not very well documented. Nevertheless they go back several hundred years.

Africa's first documented relations to China were established in the 15th century medieval days when Ibn Battuta traveled from

Morocco to China. The Chinese emperors gradually extended their power to the sea. Chinese traveling to Africa and Indians and Muslims visiting China led to a high geographical horizon of the Chinese and helped to further develop technical skills in shipbuilding and seafaring. During the Song Dynasty China established extensive commerce importing spices and aromatics to China in exchange for raw materials.

Chinese vessels dwarfed even the largest Portuguese ships by several times

Few have heard about China's treasury voyages. Way back in the 15th century, during the Ming Dynasty, admiral Zheng He guided a fleet of 70 ships and a crew of more than 27,000 mariners to the first of seven so-called "treasury voyages." His flagship was 400 ft long, had nine masts and 12 red sails and could carry 1000 men. Zheng's ships dwarfed even the largest Portuguese vessels by several times. It was a good match to the impressive appearance of the seven foot tall admiral. No wonder some say the giant made it even to America.

And yet, despite the extraordinary dimensions of admiral and ships, the goal of the journeys was not to conquer, but to increase China's sphere of influence. The treasury fleet sailed the Pacific and Indian oceans, sailing as far as Arabia and East Africa almost a century before the Portuguese reached India by sailing around the Southern tip of Africa.

Zheng's seventh and last voyage took him to South East Asia, the Indian coast, the Persian Gulf, the Red Sea and the East coast of Africa. He died 2 years later in 1433 in Calicut and the fleet returned to China. In the early 15th century the fleet was considered to be too expensive and shrank tremendously towards insignificance.

China Asia–Africa relations are not burdened by a colonializing past

Nevertheless, the fact that China as a sea power did not take advantage of its competitive edge does not mean it got wiped out of its self-perception as a power that could have expanded its territory if wanted. Today the Chinese remember Zheng He as "an envoy of friendship," who as the Chinese like to emphasize, brought porcelain and silk rather than bring bloodshed, plundering and colonialism. In this regard the Chinese just loved the witticism of former Malaysian Prime Minister, Mohammed Mahathir at a conference in Beijing. Someone in the audience asked him whether he wasn't afraid of China taking over Malaysia. He laughed and said: "in Malaysia we have been trading with China for over nearly 2000 years. They never tried to take us over. Well, one day three boats from Portugal showed up on the Malacca Coast, and guess what. Three months later we were a colony."

In 2005, China celebrated the 600th year of Zheng He's first voyage with a smaller replica of a historic ship sailing from Qingdao to Asian and African harbors. To the Chinese Zheng is a symbol that assures that China is not to be feared.

Seeking common grounds

China–Africa connections and emotions were reinforced in the 20th century by China's support against apartheid when Africa made its first steps to turn away from the West seeking new alliances under equal eye level.

All of this is well anchored in the Chinese–African relations. And just as history has formed the Chinese position, blind spots in history lessons of the West lead to misguiding pictures of the past. Maine East High School, where Hilary Clinton attended her first high school years, paid probably as little attention to China's maritime history as did high schools in Germany and Austria. Her judgment on China's current "treasury voyages" to Africa is linked to the history of the West. When Hilary Clinton took a swipe at China during her visit to Zambia in 2011 she might have thrown a boomerang. "We saw that during the colonial days, it is easy to come in, take out natural resources, pay off leaders and leave."

In the year 2015 China–Africa trade rose to about $300 billion. This is up almost 30 percent from the $220 level in the year 2014.

In addition President Xi announced that China is going to train 200,000 technical personal, much needed given African countries' poor education level.

Dambisa Moyo, Zambian economist and author of *China's Race for Resources and What It Means for the World* has a different view. She wrote in the *New York Times* June 29, 2012 that China's investment in Africa is not a new form of imperialism — it is Africa's best hope for economic growth.

By 2040 around 10 million young Africans will join the labor market every year

To manage the danger of a rapidly rising unemployment rate of the youth, Africa urgently needs to boost its economies. Any investment, private or by state-owned enterprises, any encouragement for small- and middle-size enterprises and microentrepreneurs will add to Africa's economic stabilization. Especially in countries with poor resources such investments will help to improve the lingering problem of emigration to other continents, especially Europe.

The growth of global working population will be driven primarily by Africa

Data of the UN's working population prospects on Africa's Sub Sahara working population (from age 15 to 64) will grow from 1 billion in 2016 (World Bank) to more than 2.5 billion in 2050. This is in sharp contrast with Europe. Its working population will decline from 492 million in 2015 to 405 million in 2050, unless it will allow a massive immigration or achieve a sharp rise in birth rate, which is both unlikely.

China will be hit at least as hard by demographics; its working population will shrink from little more than one billion to 794 million.

The US is a little better off. Its working population will grow from 213 million in 2015 to 234 million, still slowing down to a much lower rate than between 1960 and 2015.

BRIC countries overall experienced a strong growth of its working population. But from now on it will flatten while India's workforce will still be growing.

A gain for both sides

To modernize Africa's agriculture, China will create partnerships between 10 Chinese and 10 African agricultural institutes, an initiative that will also work to its own benefit as China has a rising demand on organic, natural and healthy products. African countries can provide superior and exclusive food for increasingly wealthy Chinese consumers. Take coffee, where boutique coffee houses offer single origin coffee with distinctive tastes.

Jinghau Lu, Director of the Sino African Centre of Excellence Foundation believes that the typical Chinese think that things in Africa are "wild, natural and culturally exotic." And that appeals to the Chinese consumer. Quality and exotic instead of quantity and mass production is just one of the opportunities for African–Chinese businesses.

When it comes to judgments about China's engagement in Africa, China is often talked and thought about as a monolith. But while traditionally China–Africa partnerships have been based on government-to-government relations, many are signed on province level. Gaza Hubei Friendship Farm for example was created between Hubei Province and Mozambique's Gaza Province.

In addition the engagement of private companies is gaining speed. Chinese companies are getting more market-oriented. They do not only learn the local language, they are also adapting their products to meet local taste and demand.

According to a survey of the US Brookings Institute Chinese investment is spread across African nations from rich countries like Nigeria and South Africa to non-resource-rich nations like Ethiopia, Kenya and Uganda. And while Western investment generally stays away from countries with poor rule of law, China is indifferent to that measure. Its outbound direct investment is rather correlated with political stability of a country.

Leveraging Africa's demographics

Good governance can reap a great demographic dividend from Africa's growing population. "Politically the model of a liberal democracy is losing its attraction," Bartholomäus Grill, a long-term African expert and correspondent wrote in his book *Oh Africa*. In search for new role models Africa's political elite is not looking to the US, with which Africa has little in common. It is looking towards regimes of emerging economies that have proven that it is possible to leave poverty behind and become part of the global economy. The hegemony of the West, its claims of moral and political authority and the acceptance of the Western universalistic view, is eroding.

"It is no wonder that the American government is lashing out to its new competitor — while China has made huge investments in Africa, the United States has stood on the sidelines and watched its influence on the continent fade," writes Dambia Moyo. And in her 2013 TED speech she said: "China is gathering momentum amongst people in emerging markets as the system to follow, because they believe increasingly that it is the system that will promise the best and fastest improvement in living standards."

In light of these shared dispositions, building the new headquarters for the 54 countries of the African Union in Addis Ababa, Ethiopia, was more than a gift. CCTV Africa, established in Kenya in 2012, is providing a new platform for China's official goals: "for Chinese to better understand Africa and promote the China–African friendship so that the real China can be introduced to Africa, and the real Africa can be presented to the world."

Without reading too much into these words they are symbolic of the change from a weak self-perception to feeling strong in the global community.

The new group dynamic leads to new political evaluations

China's new self-perception and its growing assertiveness on the global stage leads to a different evaluation of relationships. It no longer sees itself at the mercy of "superior nations" but makes its own choices.

In January 2014 *The Guardian* quoted an article of the THEWORLDPOST in which Yan Xuetong, Dean of the Institute of Modern International Relations at Tsinghua University, argues that China is at the beginning of a new foreign policy, a path of convergence, not conflict.

"Deng Xiaoping," said Yan, "gave first priority to relations with the US under the dictum of keeping a low profile (Tao Guang Yang Hui). In several recent speeches President Xi has now articulated a different strategic direction: thriving for achievements (Fen Fa You Wei)."

And Yan Xuetong adds another interesting new aspect: " For more than 20 years, China has operated under a foreign policy framework within which it has neither friends nor enemies. With a few exceptions, all other countries were essentially treated the same with the maintenance of an external environment most conducive to China's own development as the paramount priority. Under Xi, China will begin to treat friends and enemies differently. For those who are willing to play a constructive role in China's rise, China will seek ways for them to gain greater actual benefits from China's development."

Chapter Six

Mastering A New Working World

Not a Stone Left Unturned?

What do you tell young people when they ask what to study? What do you tell people who feel stuck in their profession? What do you tell people who lose their jobs? What is the future of work? Will there still be work for all?

Will the future be mankind and machines or will it be machines in place of mankind? Maybe you are leaning back thinking that your job might never be in danger to be replaced by a machine. Maybe, but most likely you would be wrong.

Looking back 200 years most people were farmers. Automation has eliminated almost all agricultural jobs in developed countries. For decades workers in manufacturing have been gradually replaced by industrial robots' hammering, assembling, welding and cutting. But all the displaced agricultural and industrial workers were not without work as at the same time millions of new jobs were created by automation. Many jobs that are a given to our children were unthinkable to our grandparents. Why would we believe that process will stop? Why would we question predictions telling us that by the end of the century 70 percent of today's occupation will be handled by robots, eliminated by artificial intelligence? Maybe that's even too modest.

Looking far into a future that may not affect us any more, is easier than looking one or two decades ahead understanding that a development is also affecting our jobs, our lives. It takes time to let it sink in. We have experienced automation in manual labor. And for some time we might have believed or hoped that replacements by machines would be limited to blue collar work. But now it has become clear that automation has entered the field of knowledge work, and is expanding to master sophisticated jobs.

Our children hardly remember the times when lab assistants developed the films from traditional cameras. Now no human assistants are necessary to analyze blood tests in a medical laboratory and no nurse to allocate medicine for patients of a hospital. Even dental technicians have to start looking for other employment, as 3-D printers are able to do their job with more precision and less burden and time for the patients.

The time to prepare is now

In the past years Artificial Intelligence (AI), and optical character recognition programs have made such progress that hardly any profession will remain untouched. It has in fact already entered our working world, we already have AI in many of our machines, even though we have not recognized and named it as such. Just think of walking in some street in a Chinese city being lost and wondering how you ever find your way back to your hotel. No problem. You hardly meet a Chinese without a smartphone in which he or she can type your question in English or other languages and get the translation into Chinese immediately. It won't be long before professional translators will need to add value to their job to keep it.

Or take a Google computer that can write the accurate caption under any randomly picked picture from the web. To do the research for this book without today's technology would have taken years. You want to know what Baxter, the "sensitive" workbot can do for your company? Information we need is literally available at our fingertips. And better than any text a video explains how any worker can teach this robot to learn the procedures you want it to do.

How many of the most common jobs in the US are in danger?

We are already used to airplanes flying on automated pilot for most of the flying time. How long before robots will be embedded in trucks? Truck drivers are ranking #13 in the US with an employment figure of 1.7 million. If predictions came true that by 2050 most truck drivers will not be humans the young truck drivers better get ready to look for an alternative. How many of the currently nearly 2 million stock clerks, the 2.5 million material handlers, and 3.5 million cashiers will keep their jobs?

China's large labor force is mainly working in the service sector and in manufacturing, many of them facing the same challenge as their American colleagues. Following Confucius words "Success depends on previous preparation" the time to get prepared to master a new working world is NOW.

Conquering mortality or causing our distinction

It is of course as speculative as it is interesting to venture into the next stage of AI.

Many scientists are convinced that in the longer run we are setting the stage for Artificial Superintellegence (ASI). Nick Bostrom, Oxford Future of Humanity Institute, already in 1998 explained ASI this way: "By a superintellegence we mean an intellect that is much smarter than the best human brains in practically every field, including scientific creativity, general wisdom and social skills. This definition leaves open how superintellegence is implemented: it could be a digital computer, an ensemble of networked computers, cultural cortical tissue or what have you. It leaves open whether superintellegence is conscious and has subjective experience."

In several surveys of AI a group of experts were asked to make an estimate what at what year would be reasonable to calculate with the arrival of ASI. The answer was that a potentially world-altering Artificial Superintelligence could arrive in 2060. Not so far away if we think back the same amount of years.

It might take longer than we expect, it might be faster. But how safe will ASI be? Can we, do we set it as a priority to make superintelligent AI safe? Given the world we look at now we doubt it.

The road ahead

Robots will not soon replace a well arguing lawyer, but they have already entered their back offices. Boston Consulting and Bucerius Law School released a study, which estimates that in the future around 50 percent of lawyers work will be done by algorithms. Let's say you are a lawyer specialized on insolvency law. Someone raises the question whether an insolvent company is still able to operate. What takes human beings days of research can now be done by legal robots in minutes. AI for legal documents can search millions of documents, read text of law and comments and formulate the answer, references included. The program, developed by IBM as an extension of Watson, is a constantly learning, never forgetting system able to search even gigantic data files. And if you wish it comes in several languages.

Algorithms are going to revolutionize lawyers offices. In the past it was the duty of young lawyers to handle routine office work. In the future back office work will be done by software robots. The positive aspect of such outsourcing is that it is cutting costs on legal advice, offering instant document review allowing people to reduce their legal risks as programs are able to check errors in contracts and break down legal language to words we all understand.

In Germany's financial capital Frankfurt US law firm Baker & McKienzie sees the necessity to adapt to new the conditions. As routine is outsourced to software, lawyers could start to cooperate with clients in a planning phase long before contracts are made and problems appear.

In Berlin legal-tech-start-up Leverton is growing fast. They developed a self-learning algorithm, which can scan hundreds of pages of real estate contracts within minutes. In the future, it will not be files and books, but laptops. The company is for now specializing in real estate contracts but the options to expand to other sectors are there.

Other start-ups like Flightright, Euclaim or Fairplane are working in the interest of discontent airline passengers. It takes their algorithm seconds to make a judgment whether a passenger claim will be successful or not (DIE ZEIT, September 22, 2016).

The list of start-ups and lawyer offices could continue. But the application of algorithms isn't limited to legal questions, it is deployed in medicine, investment, metrology and many more fields.

One should though not be too happy too soon. Considering that the 2016 Nobel Prize in Economic Science was awarded jointly to two scientists for their contributions to "contract theory". Bengt Holmstroem, Professor at MIT, and Oliver Hart, teaching at Harvard, describe in their theory analysis how to create contracts in an optimal way. Their research concludes that contracts have an enormous importance in compensation of mangers, in insurance, in agreements between public and private service providers. The invisible threats are connecting the interest of all actors in the entire economy.

Even though their theory was developed in the 1980, and is not reflecting the latest insights, the question appears to which degree algorithms can comply with all demands.

Mastering the hidden power of algorithms

Hundred years ago people were taught that God is ubiquitous and you could believe it or not. Now algorithms are ubiquitous, and it is not a question of belief.

"Make algorithms accountable" was the headline of the *New York Times* on March 8, 2016. Maybe we are not aware of it at all times, but algorithms are not only helping us in our own decision-making processes, they are also used by companies and institutions, including governments to influence decisions we make in our lives. They are evaluating resumes of jobseekers, appraising credit scores, and even more scary, predicting a suspects future criminality.

Kate Crawford, Visiting Professor at MIT and Researcher at Microsoft claims that "we urgently need more due process with the algorithmic systems influencing our lives". Frank Pasquale, Law Professor in Maryland University warns: "one casual slur about you could end up in a random database without your knowledge."

Who do you blame when an algorithm gets you fired?

This question was raised in WIRED on January 2016. It is time to think about legal intervention. The EU will set new rules effective in May 2018 which will allow EU citizens to acquire an explanation of automatic decisions and to challenge them. Nevertheless as the regulation only applies to regulations that do not involve human judgments, for example online credit applications and e-recruiting, it will leave many situations untouched.

In the US the Congress killed Obama's proposed "consumer privacy bill of rights", which was drafted based on the EU data regulations.

While our lives increasingly look like an open book, algorithms do not release their secrets and therefore cannot be held accountable. If data is incorrect or has led to wrong assumptions we have no way to correct it.

This is not just another industrial alteration; it is the working world revolution

Robots are beginning to interact with each other. We are at the beginning of a new era where "cobots" (collaborative robots) collaborate with other cobots, working together on one task. We are moving from human guiding machines to machines guiding machines able to make conclusions about the environment in which they operate. In addition to their speed they never gets sick, do not need vacation, do not ask for raising wages, and do not quarrel with a colleague. How can a human being compete?

It is not the first time "the end of work" was announced. Throughout the centuries such predictions have been made again and again. Starting with the transition to new manufacturing processes throughout the industrial revolution, continued with the introduction of assembly lines. Step by step fewer and fewer workers could produce more and more goods. Industrial robots lead to another increase in productivity. With every higher level of industrial automation obsolete jobs had to go. Nevertheless the overall job balance remained positive. All structural changes led to more jobs created than lost.

Industry 4.0 Hype or Future Working World

If we ask CEOs and entrepreneurs the opinions about industry 4.0 are mixed, if there is a real opinion at all. It starts with defining what industry 4.0 is and what it will be. We won't be wrong to call it a digitalization of manufacturing. But didn't that take place even before the term was born? Most have been in place already, including 3D modeling software, and advanced robotics. Some have not made sense for a larger industrial application.

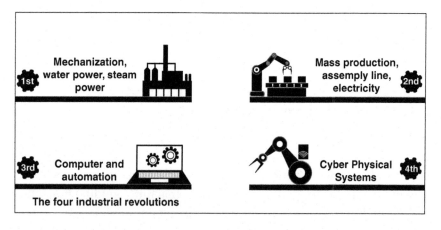

The four industrial revolutions

As with all technological advancements healthy judgment and good timing is the foundation for reaping the benefits. It will most likely be the small- and middle-size companies, which will be faster in applying the next stage of technology.

Industry 4.0 certainly raises high expectations. According to Chris Allen Vein, CIO of Global ICT Development, World Bank, "the Internet of Things can be a game changer in the world's economies — accelerating productivity, overcoming infrastructure gaps and driving innovation." But it is a process that will have to mature and to be implemented.

On the ground, among CEOs and management, we find high uncertainty about what it really takes to implement it, how high are the investments needed, how to get started, and how to get skilled workforce.

In the digital revolution robots are beginning to dismiss their innovators

The fundamental change we experience now is the transition from robots being the tool with which workers were able to raise productivity to robots becoming the workers. And, as we wrote, they are not only smart, but without claims of an employee. If we move up the job hierarchy the outlook on safe jobs does not get better. The digital revolution might hit those who were its innovators as more and more well-paid knowledge jobs are transferred to a bloodless, undemanding workforce.

Years ago after we spoke at a conference in Hangzhou, China, we visited a rim factory. It took four workers to produce 600 rims per hour. The leading engineer was in his mid-20s. However, the production line of the rim factory where identical rims are produced seems simple in comparison with producing 2500 individual gear motors per day.

That's how SEW Eurodrive, the German company and world leader in drive-based automation, sees their factory of the future.

Reality is not as outrageous as was the vision of one of SEW mangers who somewhat jokingly said in the 1980s that one day only the doorman and he would be the workforce of the company. In fact the company is proving the gloomy outlook in digital production wrong. Despite saving workforce and raising production by 30 percent the number of employees remained stable as the increasing number of orders made up for it. The future plan of SEW is to involve business partners, distributers and clients on their path to a fully interlinked factory.

Made in China, educated by Germany

Companies in China want to benefit from German know-how. Siasun, China's largest robot manufacturer bought a leading German mechanical engineering vocational school, Teutloff Training and Welding Education Non Profit Ltd Liability Company. China, already the worlds largest market for industrial robots accounting for one-fourth of global sales, is facing a high demand on robotics professionals and is planning to triple it annual robot production. To support the goal a national, high end manufacturing initiative "made in China 2025" was put in place. That will increase the already high demand in world-level robot R&D teams and high end technicians. In addition to possible cooperations with vocational schools Siasun aims to open 10–20 domestic training centers within the next 2 years.

Like Siasun, German ABB Ltd and KUKA Robotics Corporations in China are also facing the challenge of providing training to clients who yet know little about implementing robots efficiently.

To China any effort to use industrial robots is balancing out the increasing labor shortage rising wages and demographic disadvantages.

Neither companies nor individuals can rest on laurels earned in the past

The generation following Apple, Facebook and maybe even Google is getting ready for the next wave of innovation. Just think of the $23 billion enterprise of the Hilton Group (of which Chinese HNA group bought a 25 percent share in October 2016) is almost 100 years old and got passed by Airbnb, which made it to be evaluated 30 billion in only 8 years as the "worldwide accommodation leader." Nobody and nothing is safe.

Large amounts of data converted into intelligence

Take Microsoft. The company turned 41 years in 2016 and is said to have overslept the Internet and the smart phone. How could that happen? Maybe it is an example that bureaucracy can also hit in Silicon Valley. But now the $85 billion ship is about to be turned around, at least when it comes to the plans of its CEO, Satya Nadella who wants to transform the company. "AI is at the intersection of our ambitions," he said at the company's Ignite conference, saying that it will "allow us to reason over the amount of data and convert it into intelligence."

Microsoft claims to deliver the platform to implement industry 4.0. Liebherr, a German household appliances company, is developing a fridge which can identify and announce its content via sensors (which by the way has been announced in many books published in the 1990s). A German Coffee machine producer wants to use face recognition to allow the coffee machine to deliver adequate coffee instantly.

Microsoft's old goal of "having a PC on each table" has been replaced by the mission to support each human being and each organization in achieving higher goals. Like many other competitors it is working on a cloud to become the central platform to outsource all digital information and processes of companies, available online everywhere, anytime.

Tapping into China's e-commerce boom

To gain shares in the cloud computing industry US companies Microsoft, Oracle and Salesforce.com are not only competing with each other but also with SAP, the German software company which could achieve triple digit growth in its China cloud business for the third quarter in a row in the second quarter of 2016.

US research firm Gartner Inc. estimates the global cloud industry to grow to $204 billion, nearly 17 percent in 2016, and most likely hit $312 billion in 2019.

How to protect data sovereignty?

No risk no fun. Cloud computing has the potential to replace the maintenance of in-house IT management, often a heavy burden for small- and middle-size companies. But as with most benefits, there comes some concerns or risks. Whether it is data breach, the loss of sensitive information, data loss, account hijacking, cyber attacks, government intrusion, legal liability, and even if all is avoided, internal risks from sabotage by frustrated employees and most of all, careless and ignorant behavior.

CipherCloud 2016 Global Cloud Data Security Report says that "64 percent of organizations name regulatory compliance, information security standards as the top reasons for security data in the cloud."

All of it raising the question of data security and trust in a borderless digital world and how to protect digital sovereignty in a world where computer technology has become a more and more integral part in businesses and lives?

Democratizing knowledge instead of creating a new tool for an elite

In the past decades, technology has moved from Internet, smart phones, E-Commerce and social media to all industries and into production, including agriculture, education and healthcare. Now we are into the creation of machines and software, with the ability to learn. AI will be central in all we do, with the potential to empower people and organizations.

One of Microsoft pillars in AI is the agent Cortana, a virtual intelligent assistant, that "can take text input, can take speech input, that knows you deeply. Your context, your family, your work. It knows about the world." It can control the apps on our phones and our computer.

It can answer simple questions as "Do I need an umbrella?" How do I make a pancake? It can manage your calendar, find facts, files places, track packages and flights and chit chat when you are bored.

The promises are high, AI as the enabler to democratize knowledge instead of creating a new tool for an elite. The world's most intelligent cloud is supposed to offer standardized tools to structure gigantic amounts of data and make them available. It will adapt data instantly to the actual needs of clients. It will safe investments in hard and software and IT staff. It will connect everything with everything, OC, mobile devices and The Internet of Things.

But while 32 of the MIT "Ranking of the Smartest Companies" are still US-based, China begins to enter the stage.

No game without China

With around 700 million (52 percent of its population) Internet users, China's Internet market is the largest in the world. India, number two in the ranking, has around 460 million (35 percent of its population) and the US, number three, has 286 million (88 percent of its population).

And while the US market is almost saturated, China has fast and high potential to grow. No wonder China's Internet companies are booming. And its Internet industry is by far not limited to its own territory. It is competing head to head with global competitors like Microsoft, Google's Alphabet and IBM in AI. Venture capital, once rather rare in China, is now pouring into startups focusing on AI. There is a fierce competition about talent in the effort to create computers with the ability to replicate human cognitive functions like recognizing imagines and speech.

Kai-Fu Lee, founder and CEO of one of the most aggressive venture funds, Sinovation Ventures, raised $674 million to invest in startup companies involved in AI, building enterprise software and creating entertainment content.

MIT Technology Review listed China's Baidu, the Chinese web service company, as No. 2 on its list of the 50 smartest companies in 2016, beaten only by Amazon. While only four more Chinese companies, Huawei, 10, Tencent, 20, Didi Chuxing, 21, and Ali Baba, 24 made it into the MIT list, China is speeding up in AI race. Baisu was especially praised for its speech recognition which its system able to process spoken words sometimes more accurately than people. In a competition with Stanford University Baidu's speech recognition software performed three times faster than people typing text on smartphones. Baidu's Chief scientist Andrew Ng is by the way an Adjunct Professor at Stanford who joined Baidu because of its intense and early focus on AI.

When in China we switched from using taxis or very expensive hotel limousines to call Didi Chuxing. The cars could well hold up with limousine services, are on time and inexpensive. Didi, the dominating car hailing company has already bought Uber China, making steps to enter other markets and end a fierce prize war.

Didi's founder Cheng Wei believes that the first half of the Internet race in which companies raced to connect computers with people is over: "The second half is about AI."

The leadership implications of the digital revolution

It is a convergence of forces that leaders and management have to master. Emerging economies are creating new markets and new demand. There is a tremendous shift in geopolitical power, which manifests itself in the business world. The pace of innovation is increasing exponentially; new technologies have disrupted established industries and created new ones. Managing risks, complexity diversity and uncertainty paired with the constant pressure to succeed is setting the bar for management and leadership skills very high.

We asked Stephen Rhinesmith, who has been a consultant to major Fortune 500 companies and travels across the Atlantic ocean several times a month (yes, a month) advising and training multinational enterprises, where he sees the largest difficulties in mastering the challenges ahead.

In Rhinesmith's experience the real task for leadership is not limited to dealing with new technologies such as robotics and digitalization. It is many leaders' inability to anticipate exponential change: "There is a fundamental change to the past that leaders are not recognizing. The crucial fact that technological advances we see today will not progress the way they have in the last 15 or 20 years. Leaders today are faced with the double challenge — first to recognize the potential disruption in their businesses and then to understand that this disruption will come much faster than they think. The most knowledgeable leaders are focusing on their vulnerabilities from industry disruption and then preparing contingency plans for reinventing their businesses."

Stephen Rhinesmith suggests that one of the job responsibilities of leaders at all levels of organizations in all industries is to make an annual, if not quarterly analysis of their strategic planning process.

This is essential to anticipate areas where technology can disrupt their function, their customer relations, their competitiveness, or their business model.

Rhinesmith, who also has been writing about globalization and global leadership for over 30 years, is convinced that there are only two kinds of companies today — "those who know they have been hacked and those who don't." He believes the same applies to exponential change and disruption — "where there are also two kind of leaders — "those who have been disrupted and those who will be — as a leader there is nowhere to hide when confronting a volatile, uncertain, complex and ambiguous future."

Leaders today are not only dealing with articulating and maintaining long-term visions for their company, they have to address immediate practical concerns and problems. In addition, CEOs have increasingly become public figures, observed by media and bloggers, facing constant scrutiny.

No wonder Dan Vasella, when he was chairman of Novartis said in an interview with McKinsey that every CEO needs someone who can listen and to whom you can speak in total confidence. To whom he or she can say: "I've had it. I'm about to resign." Or, "I really want to beat this guy up." You need someone who understands and can help you to find balance. Leaders often forget the importance of stable emotional relationships — especially outside the company."

Rhinesmith, who has also been personal coach to several Fortune 500 CEO's believes that to master the challenges, "CEOs have be able to separate private and public life. Constant scrutiny and overexposure takes a high toll. Take critics on your work as what it is, judging you as a symbol for your company and not as who you are as a person."

Corporate learning no longer an option but a strategic necessity

Stephan Sachse, CEO of Datenlotsen, which has become one of Europe's leading backend providers for digital education solutions, thinks that without structured Corporate Learning programs companies will not be able to meet the rising challenges. As Stephen Rhinesmith, Sachse is convinced that "the agility of a company and its ability to identify and adapt to change is the decisive factor in its competitiveness."

"The time frames in decisions-making processes and measures to put them in place are shortening. Corporate actors need training to act agile and organize learning on the base of quickly distributable knowledge. Learning is no longer an option, it is a strategic necessity. The more international the location, employees and markets of an enterprise, the more important it becomes to offer corporate learning programs coordinated worldwide to avoid redundancies in design, development and availability."

"In addition increasing global competition forces companies to optimize costs. Corporate learning allows integrating learning into working processes replacing rigid, time consuming training that demands a personal presence. Thus the costs of classical vocational learning can be cut dramatically."

"*Bit-sized-learning nuggets* are offering time- and location-independent learn modules, which are not limited to the workforce of a company, but can include clients, distributors and potential new employees. Risk management and corporate governance are adding to document individual learning success, making it an important pillar of human resources."

"The drivers in that development are technology, demand and demographics. Experts estimated that in 2011 around $210 billion were spent on corporate learning, 20 percent of it in e-learning. Californian Global Industry Analysts, a Worldwide Business Strategy & Market Intelligence Source and London-based Investment Bank IBIS Capital expect the market for corporate e-learning to grow by 13 percent on average each year, making it one of the best preforming growth segment in the overall growing education market."

"Online education is influencing every step of the value added chain in corporate learning with large impact on the culture of education. It supports inherent, self-organized learning and shifts the responsibility of vocational training from the employer to the employee. Only if leaders are implementing available technologies they can a learning organization with a culture of exchanging knowledge across all hierarchies."

"The future is not a free of charge mass education but personalization and individualization of life-long education. It holds a promise for providers of elite education and for companies, which are taking advantage of it. Technologically integrated solutions allow closing the gap between academic and corporate education. How open leaders and corporations are to adapt to speed and alterations in corporate learning will be the critical question."

The Internet of the Future: Cryptography and Teleportation

During the 1980s a theme began to appear in the media: how would computer technology change the working environment? When we, the authors, got to know each other in 1994, computers had been established but their use was limited and to communicate via e-mail was just beginning, at least in little laid back Austria. Despite the slower pace of the country, books on the increasing speed of change were in high demand. And some of the described future scenarios we are still waiting for: individuals flying on tiny helicopters, self-organizing households, humanized robots and of course, self-driving cars. We still paid a lot for researchers who went to libraries and studied material only available in paper. We used the fax to send letters back and forth and were still proud to have a cell phone. The sentence in *High Tech High Touch*: "One day all calls will be free," even years later, in 1999, when the book was written, was still from true.

But while the fantasy of authors often ventured too far out serious seminars were held to get us familiar with the Internet. According to internetworldstats.com in December 1996 only 0.4 percent of the world's population, 16 million people, used the Internet. And despite *Megatrends*, which in 1982 gave most attention to the transformation to the Information Age, we were not among them.

In December 2000 that number had reached 361 millions, and in December 2005, with more than 1 billions and 15 percent of the population, it had cracked the billion hurdle. Google, founded in 1998, had gone public and was slowly making its way into home computers. In 1996, when we wrote *Mindset*, our US-based researcher had lost her job to the still relatively modest, but unrivaled search machines.

The Internet changed the way we worked and communicated. And it accounts for a significant share of global GDP and it has become a catalyst for job creation. Small and one-person Internet companies have become pillars of the rising middle class in African countries. Without the smooth exchange of data most of our global system would simply break down.

Safety, not only in regard to uninterrupted functioning, but also in the safe transmission of data has become essential. One of the key concerns of companies in regard to industry 4.0 is about cyber security when working with third-party providers and when integrating data from disparate sources to enable applications.

It might have read as an exaggeration that Stephen Rhinesmith is convinced that there are only two kinds of companies today — "those who know they have been hacked and those who don't." But it is today's reality. In all parts of life, in business, in politics and in military, the world's cyber arsenals are growing. And we are still at the beginning of the development.

Mastering big data

In 2011, Eric Schmidt, today executive chairmen of Google, estimated that within 48 hours mankind was exchanging five billion gigabyte of information (one gigabyte is a billion bits). In two days, says Schmidt that is as much information as from the first day of communication of mankind until the year 2003. Unimaginable amounts.

Wherever on this planet scientists are working the amount of data is increased dramatically. How big "big data" is was exemplified in the German weekly newspaper DIE ZEIT (October 6, 2016).

Bringing data into perspective

- CERN, the European Organization for Nuclear Research, is one of the world's largest and most respected centers for scientific research. One of its biggest successes was the proof of the elementary particle Higgs Boson. To achieve that goal, CERN scientists had to analyze a data volume of 50 million gigabytes.

- That amount of data would be enough to watch/download a movie by Netflix for 5707 years.
- The Human Braine Project is an European initiative joined by 23 countries. Its goal is to collect all data available about the brain and to recreate brain activity in computer models. To achieve that during the year 2016 alone 699,000 gigabyte of data will be collected.
- This amount of data printed on paper would reach as high as 34,950 km.
- It took two Advanced Laser Observatories (aLIGO Advanced Interferometer Gravitation-Wave Observatory).
- (aLigi) in Washington and Louisiana were collecting data for 14 years to prove gravitations waves. It took 500,000 gigabytes of data.
- With the same amount one could hold 250,000 dropbox accounts each with a storage capacity of two gigabytes.
- Relatively little data of 8300 gigabytes per month is necessary to evaluate ground vibrations which are the predecessors of earthquakes.
- The same amount of data would allow to download Groundhog Day 4882 times.

Data is going to interfere and improve all spheres of life. Already in 2006 Stockholm started to direct traffic via big data. Within 3 years they managed to cut average driving time by half and emissions by almost one fifth.

In Germany's city of Darmstadt thousands of detectors are checking the frequency of pedestrians pushing traffic light buttons and buses sending signals to their special traffic lights. Induction loops are measuring the speed and 180 cameras on traffic lights are monitoring the vehicles (without taking pictures or storing license plate numbers). All data collected allows to update traffic situation every 300 ms. The goal is to inform drivers whose speed would allow them to calculate their speed to hit green lights.

Blood as big data carrier can be used in healthcare. At least according to the promise of liquid biopsy. It would allow to spot any tumor in a body via a small sample, avoiding risky withdrawal if tissue. Special software compares DNA parts with the DNA of healthy people and recognizing pathological change.

Franco Moretti, a Professor for literature in California, leads a research program in which software is analyzing 15,000 novels published between 1700 and 1900 all stories taking place in London. A certain number of words connected with London's parks, plazas, streets and bridges allow conclusion to their emotional status. It was no surprise that London's Tower for a long time raised feelings of fear. While one could have concluded that without any data, said Moretti, we would have not known that the representation of London remained the same after 1800 even though social reality had changed.

An application of Big data that would help most people, would be an "all time everywhere translator." Already today Google translate and other services offer translation which allow at least understanding the subject of the communication. The analysis of billions of web audio data in multiple languages is the base for training automatic translators, which should do simultaneous translation for daily work within a few years.

Anticipating where the next crime will take place? Predictive policing is at least a step into the direction. The base are databases of millions of crimes of the past which allow to recognize patterns similar to those of earthquakes and aftershocks. As earthquakes hold a high possibility of aftershocks, thieves who have been successful in one location will likely hit again soon. That way endangered districts can be marked and monitored by the police on a higher frequency. (data DIE ZEIT October 5, 2016).

Big data as the enlightenment of the 21st century?

Big data hold enormous opportunities of improving daily life and work. But besides the general risk of misusing data, it's not without objections. Will marking a district as a frequent crime scene lead to a decline of real estate price or even across the board suspicion of its dwellers? What impact will highly qualified automatic translation have on the enriching cultural experience of learning foreign languages? Will the data in blood analysis work towards disadvantages for marked risks patients in their professional lives and regarding risks in insurance?

In Goethe's poem *The Sorcerer's Apprentice* the broom turns from a blessing to a plague. But while the apprentice had a master he could call for help we can only turn back to ourselves.

From bits to quits

And yet neither in quantity, nor in the quality in which we exchange information, are limits in sight. And with the next step in communication technologies safety, the large and dangerous element of uncertainty could get under control.

If we venture 30–40 years ahead, the smallest unit we talk about will most likely be the qubit, and it will be used in quantum information science. Internet based on quantum phenomena by then will be the base, replacing our current technology. (Today, in information technology and telecommunications engineering as well as in other related areas of expertise bit, binary digit, is the smallest measuring unit for information content and amount.)

The man who has the scientific capability to look that far into the future of the Internet is Anton Zeilinger, the Austrian quantum physicist, a pioneer in his field. He drew worldwide attention in September 2012, when an international team led by him, successfully transmitted the first quantum teleportation over a record distance of 143 km, beating the at the time Chinese record of 97 km achieved just a few month earlier. The experiment did not only feature Anton Zeilinger as "Mr. Beam", much more important it delivered the base for a global network, in which quantum mechanical effects enable the secure exchange of messages.

Quantum technology has the capacity to launch a new era in communication. It will allow to exchange data encrypted 100 percent tap-proof and impossible to manipulate, making data leaks, hacker attacks, bank espionage and other cyber crimes impossible.

In this fiercely contested field, enterprises like Google and IBM, state agencies such as NASA and NSA, and countries are spending billions to gain supremacy. And for the first time it is neither the US nor Russia who is conquering the leading edge, it is China. With its groundbreaking project of a hack-proof quantum satellite leap into space China is leading the world on establishing such communication lines. The small satellite, named after the ancient Chinese philosopher Micius, was launched from the Jiuquan Satellite Launch Center in Inner Mongolia's Gobi desert at 1.40 a.m. on August 16, 2016.

With the successful launch of the 600 kg Micius, China did not only catch global attention but also demonstrated that it has left the era of trailing in the footsteps of others, now moving to be a step ahead of others. The project was started in 2008 at the Shanghai Institute of Technical Physics by quantum physicist Pan Jianwei, once the doctoral student of Prof. Dr. Anton Zeilinger at the University of Vienna, and space engineer Wang Jianyu who were dreaming of finding a portal to "a whole new universe."

"A universe different from Einstein," wrote South China Morning Post (August 16, 2016), "One where a cat can be alive and dead at the same time, where bits (but actually qubits) of information can be teleported from one galaxy into another faster than the speed of light, where the Internet cannot be hacked, and where a calculator can run faster than all the world's supercomputers combined."

Europe missed the chance to be first

It was Anton Zeilinger Viennese' steam that set the first steps in this direction when he and his group realized hyperdense coding 20 years ago. In 1998 he and his group were the first to implement quantum cryptography with entangled photons.

The Austrian team of scientists of the University of Vienna and the Austrian Academy of Science are engaged in the sending the first quantum satellite to the orbit by providing receiving terminals. The upcoming experiments are the last test for a practical application of a global quantum communication network. Within a few months when the first encrypted photon message will have made its way from Beijing to Vienna, China will have made a significant claim on supremacy in this technology and also in its military application.

It is a significant step in China's intention to show the world that it can take a lead in technological developments. In addition China transfers the research results into its people's army, applying the significant military implication in asymmetric (wars in which belligerents relative power and strategy differs significantly) capacities. If China can take the lead in virtual and cosmic space it will be able to paralyze the enemy *a priori*.

In a field, where as Anton Zeilinger said, China does not really depend on such cooperation, guanxi (the central networking principal in the Chinese society), and the personal contact of Anton Zeilinger and his former student Pan Jianwei, led to the China Austrian teamwork within the satellite project. And — whether the West likes it or not, the project once more displayed the efficiency of the Chinese regime. "The Chinese government does not know long debates, preliminary investigations and bureaucratic mills. Whatever it considers as important and right, will be pushed forward with all power, writes DIE ZEIT (September 29, 2016) in an article titled *The Beijing Connection.*

It is not intellectual capacity the EU is missing, but the structural hurdles it created

When Zeilinger suggested such satellite project to European Space Agency (ESA) already 15 years ago, he found interest, but no decision was made. It is, as Zeilinger put it, "the European structural problem."

"It is not that someone was against it, but it just takes too long." Time is a luxury scientific research cannot afford. "Europe had its chance to be the first."

Blockchains: Revolutionizing Banking and the World's Economy?

Ideas, thank God, are still the domains of human beings. We all have ideas and most likely we have also experienced that having an idea is one thing, but to turn an idea into reality is another. In most cases the hurdle between the idea and the implementation is money. And the place to go to and get it used to be banks or governments.

The history of banking goes back to the 6th century BC and traces of first orders of payments in Babylon and later, in the 4th century BC, to the Greek. The Greek Trapezites dealt with payment transactions and accepted consigned money. Sweden's Palmstruch Bank was the first to come close to a central bank in the 17th century.

It was during the industrial revolution when banks increasingly stepped into the role of a mediator between private people and the economy. Private assets were no longer uselessly stored at home but enabled entrepreneurs to turn their ideas into reality.

From people to algorithms

Those of us who have been around a little longer remember the old days of banking when personal connections and judgments, knowledge of local conditions and sometimes a great deal of confidence and guts were the base for getting a loan or being turned down. That has changed dramatically.

Talking to entrepreneurs a widespread opinion is that you get money if you don't need money. Since the implementation of Basels III and IV (a global, voluntary regulatory framework on bank capital adequacy, stress testing and market liquidity risk), a storm of new regulations has not made financial services safer or better, but built up hurdles almost impossible to overcome with even the best ideas. Credit assessments are now not in the mercy of your bank manager, but in the hand of algorithms.

Now the financial world is about to face at a crossroad, depending on how it approaches the issue, either to a serious disruption or a transition. To its supporters Blockchain, the technology underpinning the crypto currency Bitcoin, has the potential to revolutionize the financial service industry, how it lends money, how it stores money, how trades money, accounts and attest to money.

Open source, open standard, open governance for the future?

Will it be a new open source, open standard open governance for the future, or is it simply distributed ledger technology, which is already existing? Blockchain as explained on a IBM website, is "shared, immutable ledger for recording the history of transactions. It fosters a new generation of transactional applications that establish trust, accountability and transparency."

Blockchain allows transfer of assets within a network. Assets can be physical, like lamps, cars, and paintings. It can be intangible like a license, a patent, a contract, a bond, and it can be digital, for example, music, pictures. In a business network it can reach from suppliers to manufacturers to distribution networks and finally the customer. Blockchains create a share ledger capability and visibility from end to end. The promise is to increase transparency and auditability and this create trust and openness. But critics are warning that Bitcoin can become a tool to illegal buys in the darknet, or an instrument to hide assets from tax authorities.

A solution to legal ownership of land and other property of the world's poor?

There are enthusiastic dreams of using blockchain technology to manage land titles in poor countries, which do not have legal titles to property like homes and cars. It code and its decentralized infrastructure are replacing human controlling instances. There is a lot of talk among lawyers where the state needs to remain the regulating institution and whether it will be possible to regulate decentralized networks at all.

In April 2016 Georgia's ministry of justice announced a partnership with Bitfury, the Republic of Georgia's National Agency of Public Registry and Peruvian Hernando di Soto, to design and pilot a blockchain land title project. BitFury's chief executive Valerie Vavilov sees three major advantages: "that it will add security to the data base so that data cannot be corrupted. Second, by powering the registry with the blockchain the public auditor will also make a real time audit.... Third, it will reduce the friction in registration as people can use their smart phones and blockchain will be used as a notary service."

The project is supposed to be launch the end of 2016. BitFury's hope is to make Georgia the place to showcase the virtues of registering land titles on Blockchain.

Bitcoin Magazine was raising open questions in its June 20, 2016 issue: Are private blockchains, run by private firms useless as they make us dependent upon a third party? Is it simply distributed ledger technology, which already exists? Or could Blockchain provide solutions Bitcoin does not, such as abiding by regulations in health care Insurance Portability and Accountability act, anti-money laundering and know your customer laws?

Vitalik Buterin, cofounder of Ethereum, a blockchain-based computing platform, believes that "private blockchains are unquestionably a better choice for institutions." But "even in the institutional context, public blockchains still have a lot of value of freedom, neutrality and openness."

Anthony Di Iorio, founder of Decentral, (a blockchain and Bitcoinn consultant service and software developer, also operating a two-way Bitcoin ATM at their office in Toronto) and Jaxx, believes that "private blockchains are a way of taking advantage of blockchain technology by setting up groups and participants who can verify transactions internally. That does also put a risk of security breaches just as in a centralized system. So you're at further risk, rather than a public blockchain secured by mining hashing power.

Private blockchains have their uses. They can be faster; they do more transactions without scalability issues. There are security advantages, and also security risks.

Resting on unfailing logic of mathematics or vulnerable to human shortcomings?

China already plays a large role in the Bitcoin world. More than 70 percent of all transaction of the Bitcoin network are going through four Chinese companies. That, writes the *New York Times*, "gives them what amounts to veto power over any changes to the Bitcoin software and technology." In May 2016, Baidu, the China's Internet giant, joined with there banks to invest in the US Bitcoin company.

The *New York Times* sees Bitcoin at a crossroad with two camps. "Populists are focused on expanding Bitcoin's commercial potential and, on the other side, elitists who are more concerned with protecting its status as a radical challenger to existing currencies."

Seeking new frontiers on mount everest and for China's Bitcoin world

In June 2016 Sir Richard Branson hosted a three-day Blockchain Summit for an elitist group of 30 people on his Neckar Island in the Caribbean to discuss cutting edge innovation, push to new frontiers and drive the future of transformational technology.

Attendees included Marietje Schaake, a member of the European Parliament, Jim Newsome, former chairman of the Commodity Futures Trading Commission and Beth Moses, aerospace engineer for Virgin Galactic and our Chinese friend, Wang Wei, who was invited to join the global group.

Wang Wei, Chairman of China M&A Association and Chairman of China M&A Group, opened his fourth Museum of Finance in Beijing on May 18, 2015 focusing on FinTech and blockchain. More than 15,000 visitors including 20 ministers and local mayors visited the exhibition in only five months to October 2016. Always ready to venture into new territory, he has been one of the early promoters of Bitcoin in China. He is convinced that Bitcoin is as much a revolution as paper money was in the financial history. And, we easily forget, paper money, after all, was first developed in China during the Song Dynasty around 1024 in Sichuan.

Maybe in anticipating the role China is going to play in the development WIRED called "the Renaissance of money," Wang Wei has successfully placed the flag of China Finance Museum on the peak of Mount Everest in spring of 2013, shortly before he organized a Bitcoin forum in one of his museums in November of the same year. If China, as some entrepreneurs believe, will one day become the center of the digital currency's universe, it needs to raise awareness and understanding about it. Despite the central role China is already playing in the multibillion dollar Bitcoin industry, too many in the world of Bitcoin and blockchain are still undetected. And yet Chinese exchanges accounted for 42 percent of all Bitcoin transactions in 2016 according to Chainalysis. To contribute to a better understanding Wang Wei and 12 business partners set up a "China Center of Blockchain Application," to support research, training and application. A second branch was set up in Zhejiang province. The attached forum attracted 1000 young businessmen and the Deputy Governor.

To further explore applications Wand Wei invited Hernando de Soto, President of the Lima-based think tank for Liberty and Democracy and one of the partners in Georgia's project and to design and pilot a blockchain land title project, to present his ideas to a Chinese audience. De Soto, who is known for his work on informal economy, estimates the value of what he called "dead capital" of property assets not registered legally in Georgia as high as $20 trillion.

Compared to Georgia's 3.8 million people, China's 1.4 billion people offer countless applications of blockchain in various fields. Worth the trip and a dinner with China's Iron Financial lady and former Deputy of China Central Bank, Madam Wo Xiaoling.

No mastership without education

We, the authors, have the blessing to have lived through the most dramatic changes and the impact of groundbreaking technologies, and we have the disadvantage to not live long enough to see how it will unfold and hopefully matures during the 21st century.

We have also seen the benefits of the Internet and social media and are experiencing how helpless we seem in its manipulating and dulling characteristics, if we do not steer against it. The only way to master a new working world and how it is working now is education. Education not only in regard to what we need to accomplish professionally, but also in maintaining functioning political structures demanding both responsible and educated politicians and responsible and educated citizens.

Chapter Seven

Mastering the Education Challenge

Education Shaped by the Past or Oriented Towards the Future

In the past decades we, the authors, have experienced the changes in demands on education from the very practical perspective ofbeing parents and grandparents of six children and 14 grandchildren. We experienced the shift from learning for life to lifelong learning. And we have been witnesses of the increasing speed in technological advancements. The diffusion of economic processes through information and communication technologies has sped up processes, making it impossible to be trained in traditional ways.

Matching minds and methods

There has most likely been little change in the tools helping us to experience the world. Howard Gardner, Professor of Cognition and Education in Harvard, has identified seven to eight distinct intelligences. His research resulted in the theory that students possess different kinds of minds and therefore learn, remember, perform, and understand in different ways. His theory says: "we all are able to get to know the world in different ways, through language, logical-mathematical analysis, spatial representation, musical thinking, the use of body to solve problems or to make things, an understanding of other individuals and understanding of ourselves".

But while his theory goes back to the 1980s, most education systems are based on everyone learning the same way. According to the individual learning styles, talents could not only be revealed but also be fostered more efficiently. If we take the very different learning styles of music and logical mathematics the difference and the potential in addressing them individually becomes obvious. While Gardner's theory has been questioned and contradicted, the basics are valid.

Musical learning for example has a feeling for rhythm and sound. It may be to study with background music (some parents including us may remember scolding our children: How can you study anything with that so-called music in your room?). To this learning type Rubik's cube may be as much a puzzle as memorizing the aria of an opera for a mathematical mind.

The logical-mathematical thinks in a different way, with a stronger ability to recognize patterns, thinking conceptually and abstractly. It can be taught by playing logic games, investigation, mystery.

No matter what theory one believes, what country one lives in, teaching can come to life. A friend of ours in Singapore is using this talent to teach biotechnologies. To nurture local talents they developed life science educational training programs. The narrative of a criminal case turns students into forensic doctors and combines solving the case with lessons in biotechnology.

In Chicago our son John turns teaching history into plays, which has to be scripted by the students. Just imagine how much more understanding students will gain of the French revolution once they played Robespierre or Marie Antoinette, or slipped in the roles of Mao Zedong and Chiang Kai-shek.

Even with a lack of reform, the single teacher can make a difference

No matter how the general conditions, the demands, the level of reform, to the students one excellent teacher can make all the difference in the world. They can encourage or discourage, awaken talents or bury them. In every country in the world, the quality of teachers is playing a decisive role.

In our book *Global Game Change* one of the chapters was about what we called the two big E's: Education and Economics. The indispensable foundation on which we achieve economic progress is education. In the past years we have spoken to thousands of students and we could feel the worries about how to find their place in the rapidly changing working world. We have met many very engaged teachers who did everything to ease the pressure, burdening especially pupils and students in Asia, on top of the list in South Korea. The same pressure is on teachers who are made responsible if students do not pass exams and if the number of students who are accepted by one of the prestigious universities is in decline.

Teachers are facing the challenge to teach for jobs that have not been created, using technologies not yet invented. Who is teaching the teachers who during their own college days thought skills achieved would serve them for a lifetime.

Where are the incentives for high performance in education?

One would think that the importance and challenge in education would make governments, enterprises and teachers work closer together to meet the demands. In some ways it seems that works upside down. In every endeavor and production field the demand shapes what is delivered. In education those who have to deliver, the teaching personnel, are claiming the right to determine demand on the basis of their will to deliver. It is not the requirements of the job market, global competition and social developments that shape education reform towards improvements and advance. It is massive resistance of a majority of those who will have to implement it. Teachers should be the bridges between the past and the future, between education and economics. Their unions, often living in the past, are tearing bridges down. The reality that even the most effective reform cannot be enforced without teachers' support is a devastating fact not only for politicians, but for all of us.

No wonder talk about the urgent need of education reform continues. And in most cases very little is being done. Good examples like Singapore and Northern European countries as models are available, but widely ignored. No wonder most of the teaching personnel resist any performance-related method of payments.

Parallel to ineffectiveness the costs for education have increased dramatically, especially in the US where at the same time middle incomes are stagnating. That of course is resulting in increasingly higher financial sacrifices of families. The same is true for China where the easing of the one-child-policy did not lead to the expected higher number of children. To many Chinese it is simply not affordable to guarantee good upbringing and education to more than one child.

No College, No Job?

Our own children and grandchildren have very different talents — but all of them graduated from college. It has become a given to have a college degree. That's true in the US, in Europe and in China. Whether this development makes sense is questionable. Who benefits if service personnel in hotels and elderly care nurses can proudly show college diplomas, but still do not earn a dime more than their once vocational school trained predecessors? In the 1970s fewer than 1 percent of US taxi drivers and fire fighters had college degrees. By 2013 that number had risen to more than 15 percent (US Center for Affordability and Productivity Report). Almost half of 4-year college graduates are working in jobs that do not require a bachelor's degree, according to a McKinsey study in the same year. On the other hand lifetime on average incomes of those who attended a college are 84 percent higher than of those who stepped into the working world with a high school diploma, let alone those who stumble along the way ending up with no diploma at all.

No wonder for years a word appears throughout European education and employment market discussions: academization.

The overarching goal is college education for all. But while higher education for all is highly desirable the degree to which it is reasonable is questionable. Professions like foster care and sanitation, which in the past decades could manage their duty very well with vocational training, will now demand a college degree. In many parts of the society academic education and social prestige are tightly connected. In addition digitalization and globalization add complexity to our working world.

The arguments for and against college for all are multiple

Some understand it as an upgrade of content, which increases the competence of the graduates. Unemployment rates among college graduates are still rather low. Others see the danger of flooding the labor markets with university graduates will lead to an inflation and consequently to rising unemployment among them. The real point is to achieve equality in access to education. The choice should not be determined by social conditions.

Looking back into the history of education we can see segmentation between the state on one side and the corporate world on the other, each contributing to a hierarchical order. Professional levels were tightly connected with social positions in which the upper class and university were as much connected as lower class and vocational education. The mental conditioning of society has not yet changed, the academic climate and the mindset of many including university professors has not indicated too much flexibility for change.

Germany is alarmed. Apprentice training positions are remaining vacant. There needs to be someone who can implement ideas into reality. In reference to the presentation of a study "Skilled workers for industry 4.0" Volker Fasbender, Managing Director of a German business association said that "To leverage all potentials for a digital future, well educated workers are indispensable for industrial and export nations in transition to industry 4.0. High school graduates and dual education have to open equal chances for professional careers."

Too many chiefs and not enough Indians?

The dual system combines school education with working education and adds to Germany's advantage as an industrial location. Given the demographic change enterprises are increasingly in competition for suitable candidates, given that to appraise education on the grade of academization of a country is a questionable projection.

If we compare a country's ranking in the global competitive index with their rate of college graduates we might see there is no direct link. Switzerland which again leads the world's competitive index has a college graduate rate of only 20 percent. In addition with $51,582 it has the second highest per capita income only beaten by Luxemburg.

Germany, which ranks number 4 in competitiveness shows a rate of only 17 percent of college graduates (age 25–64 years). Russia, which shows a college graduate rate of 53 percent and one of the lowest costs per student ranks only number 44 in its competiveness.

In China's urban regions 70 percent of the youth are enrolling at a college or university. But while China has achieved a leading position in the global PISA (Programme for International Student Assessment, a worldwide study by the OECD) ranking, its enterprises are suffering a lack of qualified skilled workers. An example is the shipyards in Shanghai where welders are among the highest paid skilled workers in China.

But while China can be proud of its PISA ranking, in a comparable vocational PISA for electronic and mechanic technicians only a few of the Chinese met the level of their German competitors.

The top ranking of college graduates in the OECD ranking is held by Korea. At the same time it ranks at a disappointing 26th place in the competitive index.

In the OECD ranking of the highest preforming graduates Japan ranks first, followed by Finland, Netherlands, Sweden, Australia, Norway, Belgium, New Zealand, England and number 10, the United States. But, none of the countries in the top places make a strong appearance in conventional university rankings.

The subject of education is complex. Education systems world-wide need structural, comprehensive reforms. And they need to move from segmentation of state and corporate world to coopera-tion between them to balance academic and practical needs.

It is an economic necessity as well as a social request. What by any reasonable analysis would need an urgent systemic and compre-hensive revision and reorientation in almost all countries is a patchwork of temporary solutions, evasive maneuvers, burdened by political quarrels, claims of interest groups, matters of prestige, lack of finance and the resistance to admit that without letting go of the obsolete there is no room for the new. Our children and grandchil-dren will pay the price.

Why Creativity Matters

The most valuable resource a country has is the talents of its chil-dren. That allows the conclusion that socially *and* economically nothing is more important than supporting their talents providing the best possible education.

But what is *the best possible education?*

Moving towards a digital world mathematics and analytic thinking have become highly desirable. Electronic information and biotechnology are on top of the list of China's most popular profes-sions. No wonder there is a general tendency that it is smart to cut down on useless curriculums in liberal arts and support math, reading and science. But how much progress has been made for those who in addition were able to let their minds drift into the unknown? How much creativity is needed to construct a car that does not only func-tion but also becomes cult, like the VW Beatle, a BMW or a Ferrari?

Imagination is more important than knowledge

Albert Einstein

Across OECD countries there is an obvious increase in the share of jobs that require creative problem-solving skills. The most popular talk on TED ever (a conference on Technology, Entertainment and Design now held in many parts of the world) was not on technology and not held by Sergey Brin and Larry Page (Google) but by the, at least then, relatively unknown creativity expert Ken Robinson. His speech raised the question "Do schools kill creativity?"

The attention his speech got might to some degree be owned to his outstanding qualities as a speaker, but most of its success can be attributed to people agreeing with him that creativity is key in mastering professional challenges. Ken Robinson speaks about well-known facts but puts them in a different context. Almost universally school systems follow the same hierarchies in their curriculums: mathematics, language, natural sciences and at the end of the list, if at all, artistic subjects. Music and drawing seem to be the first victims of cost cutting.

Students as part of a well-trained intelligence machine?

In the 18th century, the German Emperor Friedrich the Great was fascinated by the idea to turn his soldiers to well-functioning single parts of a large military machine. Education though was limited. Friedrich's fear that children of farmers might get the idea to move to cities and become clerks was too big. Careers in military, judiciary and administration were reserved for aristocrats. Invalid sergeants though, not of any use in battles, were capable enough to teach children of farmers in village schools.

The understanding that better-educated boys will become better soldiers and fighters might have added to Austrian Empress Maria Theresa's decision to implement mandatory education in 1774 in the countries of the Habsburg Empire. This was though almost 200 years after the German dukedom of Pfalz-Zweibruecken, which benefitted from the Calvinistic spirit of education, for the first time in Europe, had implemented mandatory schooling for boys as well as girls in 1592.

Nevertheless the German dukedom was about 1500 years behind the first public secondary school in China. It was created between 143 and 141 BC during the Han dynasty by Wen Wen, who at the time was Governor of the Magistrate of Shu with the goal to give access to education to the children of Sichuan. It was a house built of stones, which gave it its name Shishi stone chamber. Such a solid and fireproof house was quite unusual at the time.

About 2150 years later we spent quite some time at Shishi high school, which was renamed unromantically Chengdu No. 4 Middle School in 1952 after the establishment of the People's Republic of China. It is one of the experimental schools in Sichuan ranking within the 100 best high schools in China. It seems that some of the Prussian military heritage has made its way to China. Friedrich the Great's soldiers couldn't have been any better than the Shishi's student morning exercise where about 1000 students line up within minutes to complete a synchronized morning sports parade and disappearing into their classroom in just minutes again.

The idea of a large well-trained "intelligence machine" is somewhat in the air when one watches the ritual of well-trained soldier like students in Chinese high schools and universities getting through their training periods.

Surprisingly even though creativity is not a primary goal in the Chinese education system, in the PISA tests on problem-solving qualities the Chinese students were among the best.

But just that holds a danger. China's system creates test addicts. Any result of a test is an immediate feedback and in best cases confirms brilliance. It quantifies and evaluates. It can give self-confidence just as it is able to destroy it. China has embarked to implement an education reform that promises a real transformation. Peking and Tsinhua University are determined to overtake Harvard and Stanford. But they need to be able to break their own DNA, but just like any other country China has to overcome bureaucracy and an antiquated and inward-looking public school system. Thirty decades ago China proved its capability of curing a broken system by revolutionizing its education system. It can do it again.

The key to scientific imagination

Creativity is key to career success. In a 2014 Adobe study *Creativity and Education: Why it Matters*, based on 1000 interviews with US college educated and full-time salaried employees, 96 percent of professionals overwhelmingly agreed that creativity is required for economic growth. To 78 percent of the interviewees it was important in their career, so much that another 78 percent said that they wished they had more of it.

The definition of creative thinking was to be able to "think out of the box" and was described as the "ability to come up with innovative ideas." And that opinion is not limited to people in creative jobs.

Nevertheless science (with 69 percent) and math (with 59 percent) ranked surprisingly high in contributing to creative thinking, where the obvious artistic subjects like art, 79 percent, music 76 percent and drama, 65 percent were leading. Obvious as it may have been before, the result is that the key to scientific imagination is to support both intellectual and artistic talents.

The significance of good judgments

We have told this story before, and even as it is a single and very special case, we are sure that it is not the only talent that was in danger to be filled up by a school system that does not support individual talent but also those who fit into the common mold.

The true story began in the 1930s Bromley, England, known for a rather rigid school system. The little girl Gillian was suffering from fidgeting and could not focus. School had become a pain for her and her mother. She just could not sit still and her defense, "but I cannot think without moving," was not exactly capable of calming her teachers' complaints down. Today the diagnoses drawn most likely would be attention deficit hyperactive disorder (ADHS). But at that time ADHS was not yet the most common explanation for learning disorders. Her mother took her to a specialist. It was most likely Gillian's luckiest day.

The doctor listened to her mother's lamenting about Gillian's inability to focus, her problems with homework and disturbing lessons at school. Gillian herself did not speak a word; she sat on her hands in silence. The doctor told Gillian that he and her mum needed to talk for a moment. He turned on the radio and they to another room. There, through a mirroring glass window, they saw Gillian dancing to the music. "I do not think your daughter is sick at all," said went the doctor, "I think she is a dancer."

It was the correct "diagnosis." Gillian became a celebrated ballerina at the Royal Ballet of London and later founded her own dancing group. She was awarded by the Queen of England as Dame Commander of the Order of the British Empire. Her global fame was established when she wrote the choreography for Andrew Lloyd Webber's musicals "Cats" and "Phantom of the Opera." Today she is 90-years-old and a multimillionaire.

Einstein worked intuitively and expressed himself logically

Without scientific imagination Albert Einstein could have never stood up against the scientific establishment of his time. Without doubt Einstein owed a lot to his outstanding logic and mathematic thinking, but it was only one part of his genius mind: "When I examine myself and my methods of thought, I come close to the conclusion that the gift of imagination has meant more to me than any talent for absorbing knowledge. All great achievements of science must start from intuitive knowledge. I believe in intuition and inspiration.... At times I feel certain I am right while not knowing the reason" (Alice Calaprice, The Quotable Einstein, 2000) .

What would Einstein, who visited England in 1921, think of England today when he would get to know about the predisposition in British education politics to expel humanities from colleges. What comments would Einstein have made had he heard the Vice Chancellor of the University of Belfast, shortly before handing diplomas to young historians, say that society "does not need 21-year olds specialized on the history of the 6[th]century."

A decrease in budgets and a demand of efficiency in science consequently led to a new evaluation of what equips students to meet the demands of the modern world. Sociology and anthropology are simply considered not relevant any more.

Helen Small, Professor of Literature in Oxford, does not share such opinion: "Humanities are useful because they can put pressure on the way governments are defining and evaluating 'usefulness'."

The limits of my language mean the limits of my world

Ludwig von Wittgenstein

Fewer and fewer students decide to study modern languages. Germany faces a decline of 34 percent and the cultural aspects of literature are left to elite minorities. Several British universities like Brighton and Liverpool and Wolverhampton abbreviated studies of languages into "language courses" or "language for fun."

Where has the spirit of the German philosopher Ludwig Wittgenstein, who spent most of his life in England, gone? The spirit in which the words in his 1919 *TractatusLogico-Philosopicus* were written: "The limits of my language mean the limits of my world."

Filling a Bucket or Lighting a Fire

Knowledge and the ability to express ourselves are backbones of knowledge economies. But, as some countries have demonstrated, good education alone will not do it. Talent needs a nourishing environment to unfold and leverage its potential. When Luther spoke of "the Word" as God's word, in a broader meaning we may take it as an advice for our times: "This is the sum of the matter; let everything be done so that the Word may have free course."

One of the most famous quotes in education is attributed to the Irish Poet William Butler Yeats (1865–1939). And yet it might not have been he who formulated the phrase: "Education is not the filling of a pail, but the lighting of a fire." Lucius Mestrius Plutarchus (45–120 AD), a Greek philosopher, who after becoming a Roman citizen changed his name to Plutarch, wrote in *Listening to Lectures*:

"For the correct analogy for the mind is not a vessel that needs filling, but wood that needs igniting."

Whether Yeats had the same thought or paraphrased Plutarch does not really matter. At least not when it comes to implementing the thought.

In the past years we had the opportunity to speak to thousands of high schools and university students, mostly in China, and also in Korea, the United States and Austria.

We had many talks about how the split between rote learning and independent thinking can be bridged. It is not only a Chinese challenge; obsolete curricula and few adaptions to the need of the 21st century are a problem in many countries. Nevertheless, whether it is China or any other country in the world, the quality, or lack of it, teachers makes a huge difference in how students learn.

China–US: Teaching in two different cultures, same problems?

When we talk about education in America we are actually talking about something that does not exist. The 50 states of the US all have their rules and regulations. But despite the diversity in administration, the necessity to reform unites all states.

The situation in China is different as the Central government is orchestrating the overall direction schools and universities in provinces have to follow. In the following we are looking at high schools in both countries. And the best way to get an impression of how teaching works on the ground is to ask teachers, who are confronted with what is and what should be done in working in classrooms with their students every day. Both the Chinese and American teachers we asked are working in high schools (called middle school in China) with about 3000 students.

In the US we asked a teacher awarded as "Illinois Teacher of the Year in 2007," honored as "Presidential Scholar Teacher of distinction," became "Illinois Tennis Coach of the Year 2013 and 2015," coached Hinsdale Central High School Boys Tennis to win the "State Championship in 2012, 2013, 2014 and in 2015" became "National

Tennis Coach of the Year of the Midwest Region in 2015." If such teacher was not able to light a fire who would be?

Hinsdale High School is located in suburban Chicago and has about 3000 students. It is a high achieving school and has been selected as one of the top 100 schools in the United States. Nearly 20 percent of the students are Asian American, the highest minority population in the school. The teacher's name is John Naisbitt, and as you probably guess already, he is John Naisbitt junior, even though he is never called that way. He is certainly a senior in how to bring history to life, which is what he teaches in Hinsdale Central High School. Who could give us a more accurate, realistic picture about where the American education stands and where it is, or should be headed.

The US teacher's thoughts on education

"Twenty-first century American education is at a crossroads. Do we continue with the rote model of memorization of facts, dates, verbs, periodic tables, scientific formulas and mathematical stats? Or do we pioneer a new approach that is focused on student-led inquiry and essential understandings through cooperative learning settings? The data suggests the latter is making significant progress in classrooms across America."

"The concept of student-centered learning is not new. The emphasis on it is. Edgar Dale (American educationist who developed the Cone of experience) suggests that we remember only 10 percent of what we hear but a whopping 95 percent of what we teach. If that is accurate the old model of the teacher as a "sage on the stage" is not only dated but ineffective. Effective teaching involves having the students lead the process of discovering knowledge through inquiry and essential understandings done with a partner or in small groups."

"Inquiry involves establishing key questions that need to be addressed and understood. This should be accomplished with the students at the beginning of a unit of study. Inquiry-based learning involves the learner and leading themselves to understand.

Unfortunately too often the old system strictly involves student expectations to be listening and repeating, not asking and creating. Teachers need to be trained on how to best execute and structure this process. The result will be students who know how to formulate questions to gain knowledge — an attribute that will help them in any career they may pursue." (*Note:* Advanced work in Inquiry learning may well involve interdisciplinary inquiry. Work between English, and history and art. Looking at the French Revolution through history, literature and art and coming to an understanding based on a multidisciplined approach.)

"Classrooms in 21st century America should emphasize essential understandings (EUS). EUS are statements summarizing important ideas and core processes that are central to a discipline and that have lasting value beyond the classroom. They synthesize what students should understand — not just know or do — as a result of studying a particular content area. Today's Common Core curriculum is a product of this assumption. Like the key questions developed through inquiry — EUS are teacher-assisted, not teacher-directed."

"Finally, cooperative and collaborative learning environments reflect a fundamental shift in education over the last 50 years. For decades the norm has been a learning unit of one. Whether in partners or small groups, cooperative learning (according to numerous studies) aids students in developing higher level thinking skills while increasing student retention and self-esteem."

"The 21st century will reflect a move from teacher-centered learning to student-centered learning where inquiry and essential understandings are emphasized in a collaborative setting."

China: Shifting away from rote instructing

To get an impression of where China stands in implementing education reforms we asked a very engaged teacher we got to know during the 3 years of our biweekly column in *China Youth Daily*. At that time we started to exchange letters with ZanYajuan, who teaches in No. 16 Middle School of Zhengzhou. The city has an urban population over six million and is the economic, political, technological and educational capital of Henan province.

The school has 28 junior classes, of which each has about 50 students. There are 30 senior classes with 65 students each. In total the Middle School has about 3100 students and more than 200 teachers.

Her thoughts on what education needs are not very different from her US colleagues. During our many visits in high schools and universities we have personally experienced that many Chinese teachers, who have to operate within the established system and the emphasis on rote learning, are doing their best to help students to manage the burden of the enormous pressure of memorizing material that they might not even fully understand, especially those who are not gifted for learning by heart.

The Chinese teacher's thoughts on education

"The larger the cities the better reforms are carried. On the countryside the situation is not as good. Also the region plays a role. There are more reforms along the advanced coastal areas than in the inland regions. Computers are used in teaching in advanced regions like Beijing, Shanghai, Hangzhou, and in most southern regions. "Student-oriented teaching," which is required by the authorities and headmasters, is spreading from the city to the countryside."

"The new reforms taking place in China will surely change the ways of teaching and learning in the classroom. Now students are increasingly encouraged to study in small groups by cooperating with each other. They discuss a problem and try to find the answer by themselves through group discussion. Using this method, students can learn new things by exploring on their own instead of being told top-down by the teachers."

"In the past, the hierarchy was clear, teachers were the masters of the classroom. Knowledge was the domain of the teacher. Students had to listen to what teachers said, make notes and memorize it. It is clear that students were learning in a passive way. At the end of a class, the students were given assignments of what to accomplish at home. Now it is by searching information on the Internet. Of course, students should be encouraged to make the best use of the computer as a collaborator as modern technology has become an important part of our life. So students should keep up with times by working on the computers."

"Teachers are now beginning to change their traditional roles in learning. In the past they controlled everything that happened in the classroom. They decided what to teach and how to teach. They decided what assignments should be given to the students and how to check whether students had mastered what was taught."

"But now things are quite different. The students are playing an active part in learning. They explore new information on their own by working in groups. When they have problems they cannot solve by themselves, they turn to their teachers for help. Teachers are beginning to also act as their consultant and assistant in a way. Besides, students can study in their own speed by watching videos their teachers are making in advance."

"Some schools offer various optional courses allowing students to choose courses of subjects they are interested in. The optional courses provide a chance for students to deepen their interests and find out what they are good at, which in due course will help them make an informed decision when choosing a career."

"Modern technology plays a key role in teaching. Students can learn more efficiently with the help of modern media. Using the information available via Internet is seen as an effective way to foster students' independent learning ability. Students can turn in their homework by a push of a button on their computers and teachers know how well the students have understood. Using Iaps, students can learn by watching movies, plays and listening to materials they are learning about. Learning is done more efficiently because they use different senses while learning."

How to Grow as a Person?

A concern that needs attention in the reform of Chinese education has been the red line in practically all letters from students, parents and teachers we received during the years of writing our biweekly column for *China Youth Daily:* "How to balance learning and developing as a human being?" Many had the same question: "How can I find out what I really want and who I really am when the time between getting up in the morning and going to bed late at night is filled with studying and preparing for exams." Different from US fellow students Chinese students feel a much larger pressure from society and from family.

ZanYayuan also experiences that problem: "In my opinion, we should not only teach the children basic knowledge written in the textbooks, which certainly is necessary for them to know to study further in college. In addition we also have to teach them how to do things on their own and how to live a healthy and happy life."

But sadly, right now, despite all understanding about the need to reform, there are still a lot of problems with education in China. Teachers nevertheless attach too much importance on the theoretical memorized-based learning instead of true understanding and awareness helping adolescents to grow to be a balanced person. Besides, the students in China spend too much time working on their lessons in the classroom with little time to get a good night sleep, have a good rest and or take time for physical exercises. As far as I know, some students in the countryside have to learn from 5:30 am to 10:30 pm, which is still thought to be effective to gain good scores in the college entrance exam.

"In an ideal learning environment, learning should be just one part of school life. To support creativity students should learn how to play an instrument, listen to music. To remain in good physical condition they should play all kinds of sports, practice how to play drama so that they have a chance to explore new possibilities and find out what they are really good at, which helps them to know what careers they should choose in the future. It can also make students' school life more colorful so that they can enjoy learning as well. To master every day life students should be taught how to cook."

Education in India

How can it be that while practically every country agrees on the importance of education on the ground so little improvements can be seen?

India's aspirations to spend $1.2 trillion to build cities for 2030, with 700–900 sqm of commercial and residential spaces, and 2.5 billion kilometers of roads, are great goals. But just as much as India's infrastructure needs to be improved, it needs to improve the prospects of the people who will live and work in them. The key again is education. India's poor literacy rate of 74 percent, age 7 and above, and 81.4 percent, age 15–25 (estimate CIA World Factbook) is underscoring the need of action.

The population of India's new cities constitute the preprimary and primary school children of today. The September 2016 UNESCO report that considers India to be half a century late in achieving its universal education goals should be an acute wakeup call to move into action now.

How much talent can India afford to lose? One can argue that outstanding talent will always find its way. But what about those who are building the workforce and foundation which outstanding talent needs to successfully implement ideas and innovations.

Almost all children are born creative with a high capacity of imagination. We know that our brains differ and so does the way we best learn. Despite that schools hold on to rote learning, scorecards, competition based on mass education, it is about memorizing rather than understanding subjects. Why are 150 million children in India not even capable of reading?

May it be that the new Child and Adolescent Amendment Act, 2016, which does not abolish child labor in all forms, is supporting the idea that education and schooling can be neglected? Children can still work in "family and family enterprises."

India's government still does not spend enough on education. The goal of increasing public spending to 6 percent of GDP was set three decades ago, and with 2.68 percent of the GDP (2013 Centre for Budget Governance and Accountability CBGA) it is yet far from reaching even half of the target.

As in many other developing countries India has a lack of qualified teachers and too few well-equipped classrooms. But more disturbing are the results of a 2016 study of the GBGA and Child Relief and You (CRY) that in the interest of reducing fiscal deficits many states were moving towards appointing contractual teachers instead of regular teaching staff; with Bihar, bordering Nepal, showing the lowest share of 52 percent professionally trained teachers and Maharashtra including its capital Mumbai was on top of the ranking with 99 percent professional teaching personnel.

The amount of money spent, as has been proven by research in various countries, is not the decisive element. Timely curriculums, stricter accountability, better monitoring and better training of teachers are just some of the important measures to be set.

It does not hurt to keep reminding ourselves that children are the strongest asset of a country. Furthermore, as India's fertility rate of 2.45 percent is much more favorable than China's 1.57 rate, which is one of the lowest in the world.

Nevertheless, it is not how large but how well educated India's youth is.

What is true globally is true for India, a high youth unemployment on one side and a shortage of job seekers with critical skills on the other.

Mastering overwhelming offers

There is consensus about the necessity of reforms, even if they are not implemented. But that is not the only question within the broader field. Once the students took all hurdles of high school, the next big decision has to be made: What to study?

Long gone are the times when students could choose among a manageable number of subjects: theology, medicine, law, arithmetic, geometry, astronomy, grammar, logic and rhetoric. Over time, as scientific advances were made and new worlds discovered by explorers, one subject after the other was added.

And before the discussion about what method will lead to the best results, the question of what to choose among the overwhelming number of curriculums offered needs to be answered. At least that is the case in Germany. Opinions about what really makes sense are mixed reaching from rejection to approval.

Does it make sense to splinter science?

According to the CEH Center of University Development (Centrum für Hochschulentwicklung) Germany adds around 700 new subjects each year. From 2006 to 2016 the number grew from 11,000 offerings to the now 18,000 courses. Study Check, another study evaluation assessment portal, lists around 13,400 courses of studies.

Most additions were made in subjects such as social work, computer science, business studies, and fostering science while the numbers of basic subjects remain rather constant. One can question how much of it is fostering scientific matter, but the fact remains that there is a subject for almost anything you can think of.

Overwhelming quantity in Germany

What does really make sense? While the individual student might well be confused whether to study geography, applied geography, geography land use, geography land use conflicts, geography teaching post, geoinformatics, applied geoinformatics, geoinformatics and geophysics, geoenvironmental sciences, geophysics, geophysics/oceanography, geophysics and metrology, specifications in job offers might need just that.

The example of geography is by far not an extensive one. English language for example can be studied in 13 variables. Some single oddities, for example coffee management, were taken off the list again. Market competition and demand will decide which of the accredited courses prove to be sustainable.

It does not get clearer when looking at Harvard. The Harvard's University Course Catalogue lists over 8000 courses offered at Harvard.

"Choose a job you love, and you will never have to work a day in your life!"

"Choose a job you love, and you will never have to work a day in your life!"

The five most popular studies in the US are as follows:

(1) Business Administration
(2) General Psychology
(3) Nursing
(4) General Biology
(5) Teacher Education and Professional Development

The five most popular studies in China are as follows:

(1) Sales
(2) Real Estate
(3) Finance
(4) Logistics
(5) IT

Confucius's advice is as valid as it was 2500 years ago: "Choose a job you love, and you will never have to work a day in your life!"

The Algorithm Kings

The decision about what to study is easily influenced by the demand or lack of demand in the working world. And yet this can lead to exactly the wrong choice. Some years ago Germany and Austria warned about a glut of teachers, now it is facing exactly the opposite, leading to paying additional bonuses to teachers in some regions. There is no better advice than to study what a person is really interested in and of course also talented.

Looking at demand and supply many would wish that their talent lies in mathematics and analytical thinking. From being a well paid IT engineer to a new Zuckerberg all options seem open. And there is probably no other place that shows the gap between those blessed with the right talent at the right time better than Silicon Valley South of San Francisco.

Where millionaires are not even counted

The number of billionaires in Silicon Valley is about to hit 55, millionaires are not counted any more. It is one of the richest communities of the United States and in many ways, its future laboratory. You will find Apple, AMD, Lockheed Martin, HP, ES Electronic Arts, Cisco, Google, Agilent Technology, LSI Logic, Nvidia, Netflix, Facebook, Oracle, Tesla and Symantec there, to just name the largest of them. Most of the Silicon valley IT employees enjoy great benefits and, compared to the "normal working world," paradisiac working conditions. Even mid-level jobs like marketing manager pay more than $150,000 per year.

The picture changes when we turn to jobs IT companies usually outsource, waiters, cleaning people, drivers, gardeners and housekeepers. The good news is that the number of such jobs usually handled by sub-companies, climbed three times faster than in other parts of the US. The bad news is that the average income in this category plunges to an average of barely $20,000. Due to the high housing and living costs those laborers spend hours commuting from affordable neighborhoods.

The gap in revenues companies achieve is about as big as the income gap among their employees. Facebook earns $2.8 million, $1,412,655 million per employee, while McDonalds reaches a modest $60,000. That might change as McDonalds is turning its focus on developing and orchestrating digital initiatives across every facet of interactions with customers, including e-commerce, service deliveries and content capabilities.

Only one percent of Google, Facebook, Twitter, Yahoo and LinkedIn employees are black while of the cleaning staff 75 percent are black and Latinos. Men on average earn 37 percent more than females and 93 percent of board members are men.

For now, at least, it seems a world of white, male algorithm kings.

If we turn to China the picture does not change. Among China's 10 richest men six made their fortunes in IT segments. The 10 richest tech billionaires are from two countries, the United States (8) and China (2).

If a fairy would allow us to have a talent wish for our great grand children (yet to come) it would be informatics and mathematics.

College for all — Debt for all

Traditional education has two major hurdles, accessibility and affordability. According to an FICC-EY report, the US has one of the highest enrollment rates. India, with only 22 percent, that is, 33 million of a 300 million in the age group of 19–35, is ranking the lowest in the world. Strict regulation and bureaucracy still restrain private sector to jump in. The United Kingdom has 62 percent enrollment and China 31 percent.

With 90 percent enrollment the US is not only among the highest, education in the US is one of the most expensive in the world. "How the $1.2 trillion college debt crisis is crippling students, parents and the economy," was the headline in an article in Forbes in August 2013. Two-thirds of American students, it said, are graduating with some level of debt, accounting for the second highest consumer debt mortgages and around 6 percent of US national debt. By 2016, the debts mounted to $1.3 billion and the average class of 2016 graduate owes $37,172 in student loan debt, up 6 percent from the year before.

According to the National Center for Education (NCES) the 2016–2017 school year is expected to award 1,018,000 associates degrees, 1.9 million bachelor degrees, 798 master degrees, and 181,000 doctor degrees. In the academic year 2014–2015, the NCES US lists the average annual price for undergraduate tuition, fees, room, and board to have been $16,188 at public institutions, $41,970 at private non-profit institutions, and $23,372 at private for-profit institutions.

While parents and students take that burden on their future income there is no guarantee to finish the study or to get a well-paid job after graduation. Some of our grandchildren, who have studied liberal arts and work in journalism, admittedly these days not one of the jobs on high demand, have two jobs and are still not able to rent a decent apartment.

MOOC or POOC

Today digitalization makes it possible: merchandise not only sells to the masses and for a low price, but is also personalized. Comparable to iTunes, where people do not have to buy a CD with all songs of a certain singer, you can chose and create your own music list. And just as digitalization revolutionized the music industry, a fundamental change is entering the education sector. In 2015, in India with its very low number of university students, 591 edtech startups were founded (*Economic Times*, September 2016).

The forerunners who came about in 2008 are MOOCs, Massive Open Online Courses, education videos, which deliver knowledge around the globe in short sequences. Instead of a few hundred students in an auditorium, hundreds of thousands can follow Internet seminars. Across the world nearly 35 million students have signed up courses in 2015. More than double the 15 million students in 2014 (FIIC-EY report).

Class-central (a MOOC aggregator from top universities like Stanford, MIT Harvard, etc.) published a ranking of most popular MOOCs. On top of the list the best new free online courses starting in October 2016 was US Arizona State University's *English Composition*: Research and Writing as the most popular MOOC, number 3 London's KLC School of Design, with its course *The Power of Color*, Sweden's Uppsala University, number 9, offers a course in *Antibiotic Resistance: The Silent Tsunami*, and Dutch KU Leuven University ranks 10 offering *Existential Well-being counseling: A Person-centered Experimental approach*. Of course traditional subjects can also be found, such as Law for Non-Lawyers: Introduction to Law, offered by Australia's Monash University.

Democratization of higher education

In December 2011, Stanford Professor Sebastian Thrun and Peter Norvig, Director of Google Research, sent out one e-mail to sign up at www.ai-class.org: "This course is the online version of Stanford CS211 Introduction to Artificial Intelligence. Students can sign up and take this course for free ... All students have to take the same homework assignments and exams ... and are graded the same way as Stanford students ..." Within two weeks 50,000 people signed up for it, leading to 160,000 from 209 countries, as Thrun and Norvig explain in their video on www.udacity.com.

The free computer science classes, offered in 2011, resulted in the founding of Udacity (audacious for you, the student) in 2012, a for-profit private online academy, which now focuses increasingly on vocational training for professionals and nanodegrees.

The promises of Udacity Nanodegrees are to envision the perfect job to choose the right path, to benefit from immediate project reviews by project teams, to be connected with instructors and forum, to graduate with a credential recognized by industry leaders, to receive caried support and, if a students reaches nanodegree plus, a job guarantee.

Closing the gap between what is taught in universities and what is needed in the corporate world

And yet, despite all progress of MOOCs, it has a significant problem. According to a study by Harvard University, only an average of 5–7 percent of the students do finish their course. In addition questions about learning outcomes, rates and whether the courses really meet the needs of the learner are increasingly raised.

The solution comes with POOCs. The future is not massive, but personalized education, POOCs instead of MOOCs. Personalization is the key to deliver learning through a POOC model. It allows learning without compromising on peer interaction and on interactions with teachers and possible mentors, the lack of which is a strong disadvantage of MOOCs where you are learning as in silos. POOC can link learning closely to industries by internships, placements and by involving supervisors of companies in the learning process.

In one of our many trips to Germany, we met Stephan Sachse, CEO of Datenlotsen, a company that provides innovative technology solutions, and dealing with more than a 100 universities and educational institutions in designing and delivering digital support.

Sachse underscores the importance of involving the corporate world: "The path of a student into industry is certainly no longer unidirectional. Given the increasing shortage of qualified specialists industries are starting to apply new methods for acquiring qualified personnel. The tool is digital networking. It enables companies to actively support students from the time they enrol and it gives access to advice on what to specialise in early on.

Digitalization of education is still in its infancy, but it reaches millions of a generation that has grown up with mobile devices, social media and digital content and adaptations, they conceptualise and share extremely quickly. That supports disruptive business models in education that displace existing technologies, products or services."

Access to competency-based, cooperative-learning programs via any smart device anywhere any time as long as connected to the Internet opens a door to millions otherwise excluded for, social, financial and geographical reasons.

Connecting a world of learning

Facebook's The State of Connectivity Report 2015 showed that by the end of 2015 3.2 billion people were online, which attributed to higher affordability and availability. Smart phones and tablets are helping students and teachers to gain access to digital content and are essential tools to improve learning.

Learning has and should remain a social process. Online universities connect students. American with Chinese, Brazilians with Koreans, work via Skype and other social chats that can help each other 24 hours a day. Around the globe someone is always online and able to answer questions. This is a service no college professor can offer. Peer grading, an evaluation by fellow students, shows a surprising equivalence to the evaluation of professors and supports active engagement. Colleges have to develop strategies for the digitalization of education. Politics has to create data protection and adapt legal conditions for high schools.

Chapter Eight

Mastering Mass Communications

The place to invest is not in mass education, but personalized education.

Overcoming Mainstream Thinking and Obsolete Mindsets

Earlier in this book we wrote that in one way or another we are "creatures of habit." In addition there is kind of herd instinct we follow, not only when it comes to investing or selling in the stock market. We fall in the trap of the thought the majorities can't go wrong.

Mainstream thinking by nature is burdened by inertia and takes time to adapt. It has been proven many times that majorities and influential individuals can go terribly wrong. It always takes some guts to stand up against dominant opinions.

Today it is by far not as dangerous to oppose valid doctrines as it was for Nicolas Copernicus in the 16th century. When he stood up against the geocentric worldview, which saw the earth is the center of the universe, and contradicted it with the heliocentric worldview, which sees the sun as the center of the solar system, he stood up against the most powerful organization of his time, the Catholic Church.

144

There are few times in history when changing a worldview did not only shake up the scientific world but also ecclesiastical and worldly laws. To most of us it is not about questioning laws in astronomy, physics or mathematics, it is about questioning the menu of mainstream opinions, served to us by various media, zeitgeist and personal environment.

Structures, order and mental highways

We rely on routines to structure our lives and give order to what might otherwise be a chaotic existence. We are accustomed to thinking in patterns acquired and inculcated as we go through life. As we know now our brain is an organ that supports habit. In a very simplified way, over time the human brain creates a mental highway system where thoughts move most comfortably along smoothly paved thoroughfares. And using those our brains can be manipulated.

Studies show that most people accept a story or opinion repeated often enough as true and accurate. And now, more than ever in human history, communications systems facilitate the repetition of stories and opinions that drive mainstream thought. As a result, potentially dangerous misconceptions have come to dominate mainstream thinking, not only among certain outlying groups but also in the mainstream media, misconceptions such as the USA is great, China is bad, and the West is the driver of progress.

No wonder our starting point is usually mainstream opinion. Mainstream opinion works with strong inertia, a big hurdle when it comes to exploring opportunities in times of major change. In addition to the general dynamics of mainstream thinking our very own main stream is part of the game. The French sociologist and philosopher Frédéric Lenoir in his book *About Happiness* describes the many ways to look at the same situation this: "Looking at a beautiful landscape, a business man envisions the possible location for a new enterprise, a lover pictures himself walking with his love, a happy person enjoys the gentle hills, the colors and the harmony, while a more depressive watches the falling leaves, aware of the end of everything." Thoughts and beliefs along with our emotions shape our relationship with the world. Ancient classification already divided humans into optimists and pessimists. Our basic approach still plays a big role in how our lives shape up. The optimist sees opportunities to be seized; the pessimist sees problems to be solved.

Breaking free from mainstream mindsets

It does not take much to accept that statement in theory. Nevertheless, whether we look at geopolitical shifts or economic developments, as soon as the new direction does not go with personal preferences, we feel inner resistance. And the more our emotions are involved, the harder it gets to look at fact as they appear. To master megatrends even accepting facts is not enough. For when emotion collides with emotion reason tends to trail away quickly. We need mindsets that allow us to catch the spirit, which is behind the change we see.

On the other hand we have become too much head-driven. We understand everything that can be measured. We deploy the advancements of technological and natural science but we are often missing out on imagination, creativity and intuition to interpret and expand them.

The difference of watching and acting

It seems that sometimes it is easier to be creative in denying the need to change than to see how we can benefit from change. There is a decisive difference between knowing about facts and acting according to them. A good example of the gap between what is known and what is done is education. Despite the increasing awareness of urgently needed reforms much of our education systems are still based on rote learning and reciting. We nod to the facts, but very often we miss out on acting. Interest groups are quickly jumping in defending old attainments. We are not taking the time to look at it from a distance, detach from a self-centered view and feel what really needs to be done. Our inner selves cannot hold up with the pace of change. Inner and outer worlds are getting out of balance.

In worst cases it leads to handing over responsibilities and relying on someone else's decisions. The uncertainty of what to do is giving space to political and religious extremism. The Pied Pipers of our time are tempting with unrealizable promises, and many are taken in by it. The world ahead of us is not threatening; it carries all the opportunities major shifts offer. Freedom and choice come with an increase in personal responsibility. To a great degree, we are in charge of our lives. We can complain about circumstances, but it won't get us anywhere.

In the following chapters, we will describe the players and forces as well as the dangers and hurdles ahead of us. You can take it as a roadmap that allows you to make your own interpretations instead of being externally controlled by mounting demands and mainstream thinking. Our observations are the result of research based on content analysis and experience. It is not what we wish for, like or dislike, but what we see unfolding. Those who want to have a head start, do not only need to become familiar with the megatrends unfolding, but also develop and nourish mindsets that help us to master them.

Megatrends by nature are developments unfolding in a period where something old is replaced by something new. Mastering megatrends by nature takes the readiness to change course. And if we want to be a beneficiary of a new megatrend we cannot wait until the trend has become manifested. Megatrends can be in harmony with mass opinions and they can oppose them. The farther out the harder it gets. For *w*hether we are aware of it or not, we are surrounded by mass media and mainstream thinking. We are floating in its steady stream, lulled in its comfort.

This feeds into our tendency to search for information that confirms and builds on opinions we already have and it stands in the way of embracing changing conditions. As soon as something does not fit into our worldview or personal approach we tend to dismiss it, to overlook it. We much rather stay in our comfort zone than swimming against the stream, venturing out into uncertainty or the discomfort to change obsolete mindsets and gridlocked beliefs.

Sometimes we are not aware of the influence mass media has in creating our comfort zone as most media report within the frame of mainstream thinking. Its stream is global. And it is easy to follow. Start with Reuters, the international news agency, which covers news from around the world. Then follow the stream to your country's news agency and you will see how at first international news agencies and then national newspaper keep repeating it over and over, often with almost the same words.

Not all media delivers quality and most people do not scrutinize media

A great part of mainstream reporting uses a very powerful tool: fear. It starts with the need of filling 24/7 news channels with catchy material. No surprise, newspapers and magazine have a hard time competing with the instance of online media and social networks. The more outrageous the news is, the higher it pushes the level of attention. It is not news that only bad news is news. Many reports in one way or another are feeding fear of economic downturns, financial crisis, refugee crisis, concern about immigrants, crime and other disturbing matters. Just try to find news that build up your guts and hopes, are positive and uplifting instead of feeding fear. Whether you watch one of the many *CCTV* channels, *KBS, MBC, SBS, CNN, FOX*, Sun, STAR Plus or Gemini TV, or one of the more than 800 private satellite stations offered in India, or your hometown or local TV, read *the Washington Post, New York Times, Financial Times*, Express News, Amur Ujala, Business Line or your hometown news, available information is already filtered. Not necessarily wrong, but showing too much of the one side while neglecting others.

Leaving one detail can change the message

A small but typical example: Some months after the BREXIT shock, on August 9, 2016, ntv.de reported that the DAX (the German blue chip stock market index) has crossed 10,700 points line, recovering from its 52 week low of 8,699 points. (Still more than 10 percent lower than its 52 week high of 11,561 and its all time high of 12,374 on April 4, 2015.) The comment was that the while the DAX is climbing the DOW (US industrial stock market index) cannot hold up with it. That left a reader thinking that while the DAX has already recovered from its low the DOW would still need to catch up. In reality the DOW had already reached a new all time high of 18,622 and had recovered well from its 52 week low of 15,370, well outperforming the DAX during this period.

We are used to such precast comments, and it is easier to remain in these frames than question them. But if you do you will get a much more accurate picture of what is really going on in your fields of interest.

Even local papers need global mindsets

In 2017, Europe will celebrate the 500th anniversary of the year in which Martin Luther posted his Ninety-Five-Theses on the door of Wittenberg Castle. Luther's words "Injustice anywhere is a threat to justice everywhere.... Whatever affects one directly, affects all indirectly," could have been written today.

Whether it is the lack of education in African countries as the underlying problem of the European refugee crisis, or the focus on good education as the foundation of the competitiveness of a country, it does affect us all. Megatrends by definition are not local but global. Many new papers and magazine have got into trouble because they are not taking into account that first: information is instant: to get the headlines, no one has to wait until a paper is in his or her hands. Second: to make reading newspapers and magazines online attractive takes more than to take an article written for a print issue, and cut and paste it on a website. In addition, whether a business is local or global, all is affected by the global context of changing reading habits and how to consume information in general. Only media that takes that into account will offer the global picture you need.

One of our favorite newspapers is the *New York Times*. To understand their readers needs it undertook a research study with the following result: "What we learned was that now more than ever you turn to the *New York Times* (which ironically just changed its name back from calling itself *International New York Times* for years), not for latest news headlines but to help you make sense of a complex world... and we learned that now more than ever you need a newspaper with a global mindset."

New Magic Flutes in Politics

Many read their daily newspapers and watch TV news channels to get the most possible range of information. But at the same time many of the millennials (people reaching adulthood around 2000) prefer to move within a sphere of like-minded people.

As we wrote earlier, they move within a sphere that confirms opinions, ideologies and worldviews they already have, where their ideas and beliefs are amplified and reinforced. Twitters and likes, Instagram, WeChat and Weibo, Cyworld and other social networks are the bonding elements within "likewise thinkers." Donald Trump's followers deliver a good example of instant and constant emotional confirmation instead of fact-driven opinion building. It does not matter how many of his pretenses were proven wrong, facts were overcome by emotional walls.

Throughout history politicians and leaders blessed with eloquence and charisma could win the hearts and votes of people even if their own intentions were by far not as fair-minded as they appeared. Dazzling speakers can bedazzle. But whether politicians and leaders were honest or calculating, it took the spoken or written word of men and women to get a message across. That time is over.

Voters already not lulled enough by promises made are now targeted with a new magic flute the Pied Pipers of politics have found. The process started silently in 1950, when Alan Turing, a pioneering American computer scientist, mathematician and cryptanalyst published a paper, which opened with the words: "I propose to consider the question, can machines think?"

The manipulating power of algorithms

Up to 2016 machines could not think. Consciousness is still the sovereign territory of human beings. But algorithms have gone far to the point where they can exhibit human-like behavior. And this is not only a benefit, but also holds countless opportunities to manipulate.

Bots (software robots) are doing the job. Social bots are computer algorithms, which automatically produce content and interact with humans on social media. Not all bots have bad intentions. Many are helpful like the kind of bots, which automatically aggregate content from various sources, or create automatic responds to inquires used in customer care. The same technology turns harmful when information is not verified and when it is misused to spread slander.

A consequence of twitter posts was the early recognition of the emergency around the Boston bombing (a terrorist attack during the running of the Boston Marathon in 2013, killing three people), but in the aftermath of the attack this also led to false accusations when tweets and retweets were not verified. With all good and negative aspects, even if machines cannot think they can influence our thinking.

Manipulating opinions for business purposes is bad enough. Whether it is praising lousy hotels as great or using false statements to damage the reputation of a competitor, all can be done with the help of Internet. Fact is there is no new technology that does not carry the risk of abuse. But there is a category of social bots that can damage society and even carries the potential to change the direction of a country.

The dangerous side of social bots

Social bots are increasingly unveiling their latent underlying ugly faces. While early bots were mainly automatically posting content, they now are able to engage in more complex interactions as they grew increasingly sophisticated. The danger of social bots in destabilizing markets and politics are becoming increasingly evident. Bots were behind a company, which with no employee, no asset, and zero revenue generated $6 billion market value before it blew up: Cynk, on paper a Belize company. Cynk Technology began trading in June 2013 and remained worth a few cents a share. Until in June

2014 its shares jumped 3650 percent from 6 cent to $2.25 and kept surging gaining the attention first of penny stock gossip, then of snappier finance blogs and finally it reached a gain of 36,000 percent. By the time analysts recognized the orchestration behind the operation and the stock was suspended, the profit was gone and the losses became real.

The wondrous reduplication of opinions

On April 23, 2013, the Syrian Electronic Army (a group of hackers, supported by the government of Syria, which first surfaced in 2011) hacked the twitter account of the Associated Press and posted a false rumor about a terror attack on the White house in which President Obama was allegedly injured. The official website of the US State department of Justice Assistant Attorney General Carlin was quoted by a business insider in March 22, 2016:

> "The Syrian Electronic Army publicly claims that its hacking activities are conducted in support of the embattled regime of Syrian President Bashar al-Assad. While some of the activities sought to harm the economic and national security of the United States in the name of Syria, these detailed allegations reveal that the members also used extortion to try to line their own pockets at the expense of law-abiding people all over the world. The allegations in the complaint demonstrate that the line between ordinary criminal hackers and potential national security threats is increasingly blurry."

Bots can artificially boost support for political candidates. This was already put in practice during the US 2010 mid-term elections when social bots were used to support some candidates and smear their opponents, injecting thousands of tweets pointing to websites with fakes news.

Washington University PhD candidate Samuel Woolley and his team logged more than 1000 cases of bots to sway elections, pad follower accounts, or spread propaganda during political crises. Governments and politicians are using bots in their political propaganda. One of them is Mexico's President Enrique Pena Nieto, who has become Mexico's most unpopular president in 25 years. His bots, called "Penabots," are used to spread Pena propaganda, smear campaign and jamming activists efforts.

While to many who are not active in social networks this may sound like fiction, bots have become a reality in political life.

Facts cannot burst the walls echo chambers have build

Leveraging the power of Instagram in most cases is not linked to bending and influencing opinions but to push sales. On December 12, 2012, Beyoncé chose to promote her new album announcing its release via Instagram. It resulted in a record sale of 600,000 in just two days.

The danger of social media's ability to create and fortify opinions, hypes and even mass hysteria among like-minded people, is amplified by manipulations in the net. Social bots (short for social robots) allow buying user accounts to creating moods to support certain opinions. And it does not take much money to buy such multipliers. Instagram charges $99 for 20,000 user accounts, Twitter offers 25,000 user accounts for $145. Not a high sum for influencing voters, consumers or market sentiments. Agencies specialized on automatic postings, trading accounts, posting themes, vilify competitors or praising products can be hired easily. Algorithms are becoming opinion builders employed to influence fundamental decisions in our lives.

Dubious blogs and bought posting are building various subtle forms of propaganda, all targeting on people's emotions to influence their opinions on certain matters. Information exchanged only among like-minded will result in a distorted picture of reality. "Lying press" has become a pejorative buzzword in German political movements, but it's not limited to Germany. Donald Trump tweeted in May 2016: "Don't believe the biased and phony media quoting people who work for my campaign. The only quote that matters is a quote from me!"

There is something wrong in a system when it seems necessary to argue for diversity of sources in opinion building. We are overwhelmed by the amount of information, and it's sometimes not easy to master the dazzling array of theories, outlooks and beliefs. While political scientists estimate that echo chambers and bot net are not able to influence masses, it is said that the range of influence can be between one and two percent. In a tight decision-making process that can cause the tipping of the scale.

But, as history tells, majorities have also gone terribly wrong.

The majority is not always right

We, the authors, both grew up in Western democracies and we value the freedom of speech, the right to decide and the possibility to change course. But it takes two to make it work, responsible politicians and responsible voters. There is a lack of quality on both sides.

To attract as many voters as possible politicians and governments promise ever-new benefits which once elected cannot be kept without by adding debt, if promises are kept at all.

The sovereign, the people are acting having their own advantage in mind, ready to vote for the politician and party whose promise is the best offer. The measure of the masses is "I."

People have become used to vote for present advantages even if it is obvious that future generations will have to pay the bill. Social welfare has been a great achievement but will be hard to keep up if the number of people who receive from the state becomes larger than the number of those who contribute to the state. All getting worse by the monthly payments refugees and asylum seekers are receiving in some countries of the EU.

Already Abraham Lincoln, 16th President of the United States of America warned:

"You cannot help small men by tearing down big men."

"You cannot strengthen the weak by weakening the strong."

"You cannot lift the wage earner by pulling down the wage payer."

"You cannot keep out of trouble by spending more than your income."

"You cannot establish security on borrowed money."

"You cannot build character and courage by taking away man's initiative and independence."

How would people today react if a US President in his inaugural speech would summon them as John F. Kennedy did in 1961: "ask not for what your country can do for you, ask what you can do for your country."

If we look at the economic growth of the West since the turn of the century we cannot claim that the political decision-making processes were of high quality content. The assertion growth is the interplay of market economy and democracy under those lights is hard to hold up. But as much as idealists among politicians have become rare, citizens show little ambition to "give." Bragging about how to maximize social benefits has become socially acceptable.

Political correctness is often outstripping reasonable thinking and often used to distract from matters that count much more in fighting discrimination than just to change words.

The way out: Again education

Radio stations have discovered an instrument of amusement for their listeners, to laugh about the lack of knowledge of others. Questions like: How long did the 30-years' war last? Or: What was the profession of President George W. Bush? While of course all listeners would have shouted out the correct answer the interviewees stumbled.

How does day and night arise? Austrian high school students thought they knew the answer: "It is the earth rotating around the sun." We are for it and celebrate the new 8760-hour day!

What on first sight appears as a problem of education system in the larger context is a problem for democracy. If a significant number of citizens is not capable of understanding simple correlations how can they be able to make decisions on much more complex subjects of future of their country. While radio reporters can easily filter the answers to draw the picture of their choice it is a sad fact that education levels in Western countries are in decline. Education is not only the strongest and most sustainable driver of economic progress, it is a basic requirement in Western democracy where the sovereign is the people.

> Tomorrow's world will strongly depend of the imagination of those who learn to read today

Astrid Lindgren

Getting ready for PISA

In 2015, for the third time, East Asian countries outperformed the rest of the world in mathematics, science and reading in the Global Education International Triennial Survey, in short called PISA (Programme for International Student Assessment).

Sure one would like to know how Indian students performed. But, since its last participation in 2009, with the disastrous result of being placed 72nd among 74 participating countries. India has refused to join the survey. There are about 282 million Indians who are illiterate. And compared to China, which spends $1.800 per student, India only spends $264, one of the lowest public expenditures per student globally according to UNESCO data. BRIC nations have a literacy rate of 90 percent, India lags behind with 77 percent.

Given the goal to become an economic power by 2020, India's government needs to allocate more and better resources to education. Highly qualified Indian teachers are often taking jobs in the US and other countries. Consequently, there is a lack of trained teachers at all levels and government schools do not meet adequate standards. India needs to at least narrow the gap between private and public schools. The 2018 request to take part in PISA in 2021 will force India's Human Resource Development Ministry to face reality and set measures to improve the standard of education. If necessary steps are taken, there is no reason Indian students could not catch up with the best students in the world.

Countries need responsible voters

Sadly, in many countries of the West, reading competence, the ability to read, process and understand the meaning of a script, is in decline. And this does not just have implications on professional life but also on the political matureness of the people of countries. Just imagine an election day where people vote indirectly for the future financial architecture of their country. Or whether Transatlantic Trade and Investment Partnership (TTIP) and Comprehensive Economic and Trade Agreement (CETA) make sense. What are the lenses through which to judge? Personal advantage and disadvantage? A certain industry's interest? The interest of a profession, let's say lawyers? The future of the children or the country?

How to get neutral information? How to evaluate biased information? It is very hard to get a clear picture. That's why we elect parliaments and politicians to represent us in questions and decisions important for the country as a whole but difficult to evaluate with the average level of information people usually have. But to decide who will represent the people in making such decisions citizens need to be able to make reasonable judgments of who to give their vote. And to make such judgments we need a foundation, which is again, education.

How does one, if to process and understand the meaning of a script is a problem, follow election speeches? How much more of a problem is scrutinizing content when the words are spoken and one cannot be stopped, read twice or slowed down the speed. The lower the education level, the higher the danger of wrong decisions we later regret. Confucius connected understanding and the value of wisdom: "By three methods we may learn wisdom: First, by reflection; that is the noblest: second by imitation, which is the easiest; third by experience, which is the bitterest."

Chapter Nine

Mastering A New Trade Order

The Creation of a Megatrend

The total amount of global merchandise trade in 2015 reached 16.5 trillion (WTO). What will be the impact of a new trading route with an estimated trade volume of more than $2.5 trillion embracing about 65 percent of the world's population, about one-third of the world's GDP and about one quarter of all goods and services moved globally?

All of this in times when global trade slowed down from 7 percent growth it reached per year before the 2008 financial crisis to 1.5 percent in 2015 and 2016.

Many have heard about the project. Few are familiar with it. We are talking about China's 21st century project, President Xi's signature assignment, the "One Belt One Road Initiative." To realize such a vast project is not mastering a megatrend, it is creating one.

One Belt One Road (OBOR) with a pledged completion by 2025 will become an engine for China's growth and it will feed the demand of developing neighbors and provide infrastructure to the regions along its routes. The aim is to create an unblocked road, rail and ship network between China, Asia, Europe, Africa and in the longer-term extension, Latin America. One goal is to shorten the time of bulk consumer goods transports to Europe and it will include at least one high-speed railroad reaching 320 km/h. It is expected to cut overland travel from Beijing to London to just two days. In 2016 it takes 15 days.

Here are five questions the project raises:

1. What does One Belt One Road stand for?
2. What are its historical roots?
3. How will it be funded?
4. Why is it most likely to reach its goal?
5. Why it is important to business globally?

India's questions are of a very different kind

Despite all global attention and despite grand attributes as "the number one project under heaven, " India's position towards China's Belt and Road Initiative remains skeptical and cautious. India's Foreign Secretary sees China's OBOR as an instrument to increase influence.

India's history gives all reason for mistrust. In the past 60 years, India has been at war with both neighbors, Pakistan, a strong supporter of OBOR, and with China. The China–Pakistan Economic Corridor runs through Pakistan-occupied Kashmir and Gilgit–Baltistan, Indian territories as understood by Delhi. This and the lack of detailed operational plans remain as baggage for a more positive approach to China's OBOR plans. In short, without consultation and integrating India into its Belt and Road Initiative, a larger buy in from Delhi does not seem within reach.

While India in short term will not endorse OBOR, it will expand its economic engagement with China and Asia. China–India trade increased to more than $70 billion in 2016. India also has strong engagement in ASEAN, which will benefit from OBOR projects just as in East and West Africa.

Independent of any political consideration OBOR will hold potential business. International competitive bidding, supported by a stricter format of AIIB, hold opportunities for Indian companies for work and service contracts, particularly in energy, water and supply of goods.

OBOR is part of China's "going out" policy. But there is a gap between words and deeds. China has a lot of space to improve on working visas, regulatory permits and various requirements for foreign businesses. Indian enterprises would like to see China taking down hurdles for registration processes of Indian pharmaceutical companies. Another complaint is the favoring of Chinese local and state-owned companies in competing for contracts. This stands in the way of confidence and trust-building processes.

A more balanced and relaxed business climate would be in the interest of both Indian and Chinese entrepreneurs. But whether an economic India–China dialogue will lead to mid-term results or not, a better understanding of China's OBOR plans is useful and accessible to all.

What does One Belt One Road stand for?

One Belt One Road is the slightly confusing name for several trading routes on land and by sea. On first sight One Belt One Road Initiative is a gigantic infrastructure project that will allow business to operate along its various routes, with the potential to also become the most likely largest platform for regional cooperation. China's strategy is "to align and coordinate the development of the countries along the Belt and Road, foster market potential, promote investment and consumption and create demands and job opportunities."

The "Belt," which encompasses the 21st century Maritime Silk Road, are shipping lines leading from China's coast through the South China Sea and the Indian Ocean to ports in Europe, and through the South China Sea and the South Pacific to ports in Asia and Africa.

In the Chinese understanding the character for Belt does not only stand for a physical belt but also for connecting and bonding. By the official statements, beside its economic goals, the purpose of One Belt One Road is to: "deepen political trust; enhance cultural exchanges; encourage different civilizations to learn from each other and flourish together; and promote mutual understanding, peace and friendship among people of all countries."

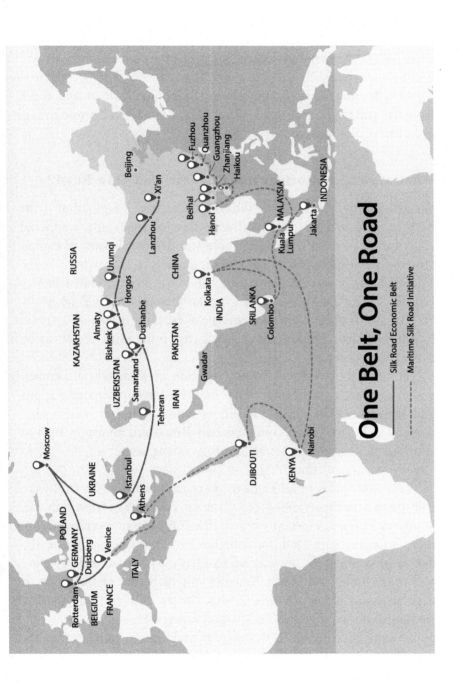

One Belt, One Road

—— Silk Road Economic Belt

----- Maritime Silk Road Initiative

"It covers, but is not limited to, the area of the ancient Silk Road. It is open to all countries, and international and regional organizations for engagement, so that the results of the concerted efforts will benefit wider areas."

One Road stands for the physical landlines, which will reach from Central China through Central Asia, Russia and Europe ending up north in Scandinavia.

What are the historical roots of One Belt One Road?

When most people think of the Silk Road, the imagination drifts back to ancient times. Men with long flowing robes in the imperial court full of peacocks, nomad people and desert caravans of camels crossing from China to their destination maybe somewhere in the Middle East. It was formally established during the Han Dynasty (206 BC–220 AD) and was used regularly from 130 BCE when the Han began to officially trade with the West until it was interrupted by the Ottoman Empire which boycotted trade with the West by closing the routes.

The romantic image is a simplification of what was a complex and integrated set of trading routes and relationships among nations and kingdoms. The desire for silk as luxury material was in high demand in Egypt, Greece and especially Rome and allowed China to establish a position as textile manufacturing center of the world already in ancient times.

Teas and spices of all kinds of preventive health properties were transported on the so-called Tea Caravan Trail. It ran from Jinhong, Southern Yunnan, especially known for cultivating Pu-erh tea. From there it led through Dali, the kingdoms of Dali Lijiang, Mosu, the nation of women, all the way up to Lhasa, to Xigaze to Darjeeling and on to India. As South Asia did not plant tea at that time, it depended on Chinese tea, and in turn, the tea caravan trail. Another trading route led through Turkey and Eastern Europe and was predominantly used by Arab traders. Of much more impact than tea and silk was paper, which was invented during the Han dynasty, and of course gunpowder.

With its complex network of major cities, many of which achieved very high levels of science and art the greatest value of the Silk Road was the exchange of culture and art, philosophy and religion. One example is Buddhism, which entered China in a massive way during the Tang Dynasty. As the story goes it was a Buddhist monk Xuanzang, who traveled to India bringing back Sutras which led to building the Great Wild Goose *pagoda* which can still be visited in Xian. Astronomy research reached the highest level of the time in the cities of Isfahan, Samarkand, and Lhasa.

Probably very few know that the motto United States Postal Service, inscribed on New York's James Farley Post Office, goes back to the Persian Royal Road, one of the main arteries of the ancient Silk Road. It was taken from the writing of Herodotus (480–429 BCE), a Greek historian and contemporary of Socrates. Impressed by the speed and efficiency of the Persian messengers he wrote: "Neither snow, nor rain, nor heat, nor darkness of night prevents these couriers from completing their designated rounds with utmost speed."

The ancient silk trading route where globalization, in its true sense, really began, started long before the Tang Dynasty. It became the established economic order and was only disrupted by colonialism in the beginning of the 19th century. In the total narrative of human history, this economic order had a temporary disruption of a mere 150 years.

The collective unconscious of people, from China, Korea, Pakistan, Afghanistan, Turkistan, Turkmenistan, crossing Central Asia into the Middle East into East Africa and North Africa, holds the idea of revitalizing the Silk Road as an economic trading community. It's not about establishing something new.

Looking at the new Silk Road in its historic context it is not only establishing a *new* trade order changing the world's economic relations. It reaches far deeper. In the Chinese mindset it is bringing back what was always there.

Keeping the momentum of growth

Looking back at three decades of South and North East Asia's economic development the share of manufacturing in GDP crossed

25 percent in South East Asia and 30 percent in North East Asia. In the tail of the rapid growth of manufacturing employment rate and productivity rose.

At the same time improvements were made in the skills of workers by better training of management and increasingly global thinking entrepreneurs. But despite all the achievements export-processing trade has declined. Total exports of China fell to minus 2.9 percent in 2015 and minus 7.1 percent in the first half of 2016 (HKTDC Research).

It has been clear to China that to keep the momentum in economic growth it has to transform its economy from manufacturing-driven to a more consumption-driven and service-driven model. And it has to search for new markets.

China will follow what has fueled its own growth on the past decades, building infrastructure. Anyone who travels China is quite taken by its high-speed train network, the light-flooded railway stations and the many brand new airports, which connect China's cities with each other and with the world. Building infrastructure was core in building today's China. It is a goal of One Belt One Road to replicate this in many of the emerging economies along the 21st century Silk Roads.

How will One Belt One Road be funded?

In the year 2015 China's outbound investments reached nearly $120 billion. But even such deep pockets reach their limits. Who Will Pay for Asia's $8 Trillion Infrastructure Gap?" was the headline of an Infographic of the Asian Development Bank on September 2013. The article estimated that $8 trillion were needed between 2013 and 2020 to fund infrastructure construction for Asia. Infrastructure is needed to lift people out of poverty. More than 60 percent of households in developing countries in Asia are without access to drinking water and modern sanitation. More than 50 percent of the people see jobs or business as the best way to get out of poverty. Building the necessary infrastructure along the route is the basic condition for the private sector to add its dynamics and resources.

To finance OBOR investments, three financial institutions have been set up to support its development.

Silk Road Infrastructure Fund: The $40 billion fund was launched in February 2014 and will invest in One Belt One Road infrastructure projects. It is capitalized mainly by China forex reserves and is projected to be managed like China's sovereign wealth fund. The fund's Chief Executive is Ms. Jin Qi, former assistant to the People's Bank Of China (PBOC) Governor.

Asian Infrastructure Investment Bank: AIIB was founded as a multilateral development bank in October 2014 with a registered capital of $100 billion. Despite resistance led by the US it has 57 members and is led by Jin Liqun, former Chairman of China International Capital Corporation, Vice President of the Asian Development Bank. AIIB will focus on the development of infrastructure and other productive sectors in Asia, including water supply and sanitation, environmental protection, urban development and logistics.

New Development Bank (NDB): NDB is a BRICS multilateral development bank established on July 2014. The founding members are Brazil, China, India and Russia and South Africa. The initial capital was $50 billion with the intention to increase capital to $100 billion. The bank will fund projects in developing countries and foster global, regional and local partnership with new and established Multilateral Development Banks (MDB). It is led by K.V. Kamath, former Chairman of Infosys Limited, India's second largest IT services company.

Singapore's state-owned development boards will partner with China Construction Bank committing around $22 billion to OBOR. The first capital installment of $10 billion was made by 5 percent China Development Bank, 15 percent Export–Import Bank of China, 15 percent China Investment Corporation, 65 percent State Administration of Foreign Exchange.

China's vision of the "Silk Road Economic Belt" is not limited to Asia but aims to create an integrated network of communications and transportation that will facilitate investment and development across Asia, Europe, Africa.

Why is One Belt One Road most likely to reach its goal?

One Belt One Road is about business, not charity. It's about building infrastructure to allow business to operate. And it's about a new challenge, which China itself is facing, and that is smart infrastructure — ecologically sound infrastructure. Understanding the integration of water and food systems with the environment and realizing that too much industrial growth does not necessarily equal a healthy economy.

These are all factors coming together and converging in the creation of a new economic paradigm, which has as its skeletal framework the One Belt One Road, but it is much bigger than the One Belt One Road. It is involving a new consensus of ideas around economic development, and also an evolution of a consensus of ideas about political ideology, meaning non-interference, non-alignment, without necessarily any one Western or dominant power, and seeking exchange of experiences rather than trying to force one model on anyone else.

That's really the difference of what's emerging and that's why China is getting so much synergy and momentum.

China's six domestic reasons

In China's One Belt One Road Initiative six domestic strategic pillars will play key roles:

1. Diversify the Chinese economy and go outbound
2. Make Funds available
3. Coordinate investment by region
4. Building on understanding each other
5. China is taking *guanxi* on a global stage
6. Leapfrog Infrastructure

Diversify the Chinese economy and go outbound

China's OBOR is taking place parallel with a restructuring of the Chinese domestic economy. China embarked on a policy of hypergrowth, which lasted for a decade and a half a large part of economic growth was achieved by infrastructure and construction. But now it has reached a crossroad in its economic development. The question is where do they go next. To sustain growth China's strategy is to transform to a productivity-led, technology and services-oriented economy, which in due course will help to move from an export-driven market to domestic consumption. China has, in fact, inflated its own labor costs. This is due to a great extent fixed-asset investments focusing on real estate, and real-estate prices were driven up. This in turn has driven up labor costs and in addition to lower demand enormous overcapacities have been mounting. In parallel improvements on labor rights made China less cost-effective. Some investments are going elsewhere.

China has to find a way to diversify its domestic economy as well as going outbound. The decision is complex. China is investing outside of the nation's borders but does not wish to follow the path of American corporate multinationals outsourcing everything, leaving its own nation with diminished capacity or capability of producing anything at the end.

As a result China is looking at linkages and comparative advantages with neighboring countries and building an entire network of associated growth regions across the OBOR and the nations of the Global Southern Belt. OBOR will support exporting commodities such as steel, provide workforce and engage engineers not needed in China. By investing into the infrastructure for other nations, exporting labor, materials and technology, China's economy in turn will benefit and build up on economic resilience.

In addition its investments in infrastructure will lay foundations for manufacturing encouraging the private sector to follow, invest and create jobs, not only for local people but also for Chinese going overseas to run the businesses.

Making funds available

China is willing to give other countries "a ride" as President Xi confirmed in August 2016 (*China Daily*, August 18, 2016). According to the official statement of the Silk Road Fund, the philosophy behind investments is to make investment decisions based on market principles, international practice and professional standards. Investments will be made in equity, debt and in other funds working jointly with domestic and overseas financial institutions to set up funds, manage entrusted assets and commission others to invest.

Funds will be made available to support trade, economic cooperation and connectivity within the Belt and Road Initiative. To promote common development of China and the countries and regions participating in the Belt and Road Initiative china is collaborating with domestic and international enterprises and financial institutions.

To meet its strategic goals to push forward industrialization and stabilize the world economy, the fund will be directed and controlled by a board of directors, supervisors and a management team. To set up effective and efficient corporate governance mechanisms the fund has also engaged high-profile professionals with various backgrounds.

Coordinate investment by region

In an OBOR communication project with students of Beijing Foreign Studies University we have experienced first hand China's ambition to train students in foreign languages as a base for diplomatic and economic goals. Approaching people in their own language is part of China's going global strategy. Take Sri Lanka as an example: Up to now Chinese companies have invested more than $5 billion building roads, power plants, harbors and hotels. More than 30,000 Chinese are working in Sri Lanka.

China has managed to build up a new relationship in the Arab world without disturbing its good relationship with Israel. In 2015 China bought the license to run Israel's largest harbor in Haifa, it builds a new terminal for ultra-large containerships in the second largest harbor, in Aschdod, and cofinances and builds a land bridge from there to Israel's third largest harbor in Eilat at the Red Sea.

Or take Kazakhstan. Its rich energy reserves brought economic growth and rising income for its population and some extravagance for the long-term President, Nasarbajew. Since the fall of oil prices its strategic partnership with China and its positioning in the economic corridor and the railway link opened new doors of opportunity. Chinese companies now own close to one quarter of Kazakhstan's oil production.

In Turkmenistan, which between 2009 and 2015 exported 125 billion cubic meters of gas to China, CNPC is now developing Bagtyyarlyk gas, after commissioning Bota, Tangiguyi and Uzyngyi gas fields. And it has recently signed a $15 billion in gas and uranium deals with Uzbekistan. These are just some examples for China's geostrategic investments.

But China is not only strengthening relations in emerging economies of Asia and Africa. It reaches out to European OBOR countries. It is financing the Greek port of Piraeus and the $3 billion bullet train from Belgrade to Budapest. Rairoads, pipelines and roads will be built from Xian to Belgium and a 8000 mile cargo rail route from Yiwu (about 100 km south of Hangzhou) to Madrid.

Building on understanding each other

The ancient Silk Road was not only about trading silk and tea. It was also about the complex exchange of goods, ideas and culture. It was the juxtaposition and integration of many cultures. One Belt One Road will play a key role in enhancing China's communication capacity, and as President Xi said, "will strengthen its voice and tell China's story well."

Not too many in Western Europe may have heard of the 16+1 group created in 2011 by China and 16 Eastern and Central European countries: Albania, Bosnia and Herzegovina, Bulgaria, Croatia, Czech, Estonia, Hungary, Latvia, Lithuania, Macedonia, Montenegro, Poland, Romania, Serbia, Slovakia and Slovenia. The formula 16+1 stands for an initiative of intensifying cooperation among 11 EU member states and five Balkan countries. It includes not only infrastructure but also education science and culture.

A 5-year exchange program for 1000 young people from China and the 16 European countries has been created to enhance people-to-people communications and gain a better communication base for future opinion leaders.

Building infrastructure is part of China's success story. Emphasizing infrastructure has to do with its own developmental experience to strategically connect things in order to grow an economy. This is the framework.

The broader economic paradigm is to revitalize South–South cooperation, South–South experience exchange among the nations we collectively call the Global Southern Belt. In working together having faced the same challenges in colonial and post-colonial era is a bonding element! Sharing the challenges of dealing with diverging economic conditions within country borders, bridging the gap between advance high-tech clusters and outworn production. And in addition, now more urgent than ever before, taking into account environment considerations, issues of water, food and health security.

The experiences of China and the experiences of South China, India, Pakistan and Kazakhstan may be very different but there are certain experiences that are similar because they are coming from a certain baseline of underdevelopment, colonialism, in the case of some, having been under the Soviet Union, having a kind of imperial communist experience, getting out of socialism, moving toward the market. In other cases it is digesting the past of capitalism under a colonial exploitation and get out of aid-based or aid-dependent development.

China's own example of helping African countries when it was itself was still one of the poorest countries is not forgotten. It gives China credibility and adds to the guidance what its own history of pragmatic, business-like approach to develop a country offers.

In addition to building on ancient bonds Chinese has developed a strategy to address people in their mother tongue. CCTV has become a significant 24/7 information channel addressing people in local languages, in addition to English, in French, Spanish, Arabic and Russian.

China is taking *guanxi* on a global level

China's One Belt One Road initiative is not only about economics. It is building bridges across different cultural backgrounds. It's about getting to know each other and building up friendship and trust. To reach that stage is a goal worth every effort even if the hurdles are very high. From the Western point of view China and its signature One Belt One Road Initiative are still seen in two ways: as a project of conquering the world and as the largest boom project ever.

China's diplomatic effort to build friendly relations, or in other words, to take *guanxi* on a global level, is an effective tool in taking down barriers. Nevertheless is it not easy to address people in their cultural and emotional language. There is still much room to improve. The stakes are high, but if China takes its own experience and extends it globally across the countries along the maritime and the landlines of the new Silk Roads it needs to speak in both the literal and the emotional language of a country.

Leapfrogging infrastructure and technology

While China has become a master in "crossing the river by feeling the stones" in some matters the strategy to choose is to leapfrog in technology and platforms. Implementing for example the newest infrastructure technology instead of modernizing gradually.

We do not have to go to Africa to see the need of improving infrastructure. As part of the China-Central and Eastern European Countries partnership (CEEC) the first concrete project has been signed between China, Hungary and Serbia on the development, construction and financing of the 350 km Hungary–Serbia high-speed train.

China plans to invest $720 billion on 303 transport infrastructure projects between 2016 and 2019. The amount sounds enormous but it has to be put in relation with the enormous size of the country. "China spends more on economic infrastructure annually than North America and Western Europe combined," Bloomberg quoted a Chinese report in June 2016. The number of Chinese airports has increased from 148 in 2007 to a planned 240 in 2020. During the same period expressways will grow from 54,000 km to 139,000 km. With such unprecedented capacity and experience China already has laid more than 12,000 miles of railroad tracks, more than the rest of the world combined. High-speed rail networks will connect China with all of South Asia.

In the developing business opportunities along the various land and maritime routes of OBOR China will leapfrog into a new working world in which robotic, self-drive systems and digital production are the driving forces.

In an interconnected world it will be easier to bundle its creative potentials. Borders are fading economically not only among countries but also between employment and self-employment. For the past decades China has held its learning capacity very high. There is no reason it would change that mindset.

Green Finance in a Green Silk Road

Most of the 70 countries along the route are emerging economies. Most of them are in the process of industrialization and urbanization, but without the indispensable infrastructure to support economic development. Many of these nations depend heavily on energy and mining industries. Many of the countries along the Belt and Road have similar geographic and economic conditions; some already have frequent trade exchanges. Their common goal for growth raises the question of how to achieve a balance between boosting developments while at the same time paying attention to the ecology between economic and ecological benefits.

Avoiding the approach to make a mess first and clean up later

To avoid the struggle between economic and ecological benefits and to meet the expectations of the people along the regions and countries of Silk Road, China wants to contribute to build a

"Green Silk Road," by promoting green finance and green development supported by regional collaboration.

The concept of an eco-civilization and green development are important parts of the Belt and Road Initiative. Well aware of its own approach from the past, "of making a mess first and clearing it up later," China understands the importance of moving away from one-sided massive-scale development pushing environmental considerations aside. To minimize environmental damage China is willing to explore cooperation models with emphasis on both economic and ecological benefits.

China's Silk Road Fund announces implementation of green development and green finance in projects of the global green transformation movement, which will include major new energy, green transport, environmental governance and various other infrastructure projects.

Green projects need large investments for low initial payback

Infrastructure investment in emerging markets bears a lot of risk and sometimes takes a long time and risks until it pays off. One of the large advantages of OBOR funds is the ability and willingness to provide reasonable financing terms for green projects despite long construction and return cycles, huge capital needs and low initial payback.

Only projects which evaluate social, economic and environmental benefits of an investment will ensure stable development along the Silk Roads. What is needed is nations which use funds for investments can solve problems that inhibited progress in the past.

Within China's push for a Green Silk Road, China's green industries, including clean energy and advanced equipment manufacturing industries, the Fund will support their efforts to export advanced technologies to support green development in the countries along the route. To promote greater resource productivity and to reduce waste, Chinese enterprises will be able to purchase advanced green technologies such as garbage treatment and advanced chemical technologies. The goal is to save energy, reduce emissions and build a circular economy along the Green Silk Road.

Possibly the world's largest platform for collaboration

Trade routes will not only change in Asia, One Belt One Road has the potential to transform trade globally. While there are still many economic and political hurdles to take, and misuse of funding prevented, it has already exceeded its planning phase. Leading financial and construction companies are getting involved. You have optimism and pessimism in whether OBOR will reach its proposed geographic coverage, economic goals and possible financial returns.

There is no guarantee. But if we consider what is at stake for China the minimum one must do is to watch its development carefully.

Chapter Ten

Mastering Our Thoughts

The Power of Not Having to be Right

Theodore Roosevelt, 26th President of the United States from 1901 to 1909, formulated it simply: "Unless a man is master of his soul, all other kinds of mastery amount to little."

When it comes to mastering megatrends, few mindsets are more important to understand the power of liberating yourself from having to be right. Just think about this: If you talk about your left side to someone opposite to you it is your right side. The direction depends on the point of reference. The same principle can be applied to opinions and beliefs. Our truth is subjective because true is what appears to be true to us.

It is worth while to dedicate some time thinking about how open our mind is in questioning an opinion we hold on to or a statement we adopt because we like to hear it. To be aware of the relativity of "the truth" is key when it comes to mastering our thoughts rather than being driven by our thoughts and emotions. That's the precondition to coming to conclusions that allow us to make the most of our environment and of megatrends that will have an impact on it. And while it sounds like an obvious characteristic to have, reality shows for many it is hard to act that way.

What is "the truth?"

Natural laws, history and on smaller scales, rules for upbringing, education, health, cultural and sexual behavior have been rewritten many times. "Where do we come from?" "Why are we here?" "Where do we go to?" are not only the themes of the most famous painting of the French painter Paul Gauguin, but also fundamental philosophical questions.

Depending on who we ask those questions it will be answered in many different ways. But no matter how convinced various sides are no one will be able to claim to own the absolute truth. We do not have to stress religion to get to the insight that there is no such thing as one truth for all. Nor can we claim infinitive truth on insights.

Nevertheless to own the "right answer" is a common claim separating religions and ideologies. Endless TV discussions are hosting people who offer and often fiercely defend their "right answer." Left wing, right wing, pro-free market, against-free market, pro-more bank regulations, less interference of the state, more government, less government, the list could fill a book.

And then there are the daily quarrels about more or less nothing except quarreling who is right, often forgetting what the matter in dispute has originally been. How much energy is wasted without any feasible result. To have an opinion is important, but to allow an opinion to be put in question means to add value to the view.

Mastering Megatrends is Linked to the Willingness to Change with New Information Available

Confucius in the 5th century BC taught that: "Real knowledge is to know the extent of one's ignorance."

And the American 19th century humorist Henry Wheeler Shaw said bluntly: "There are two kinds of fools: those who can't change their opinions and those who won't."

In *Megatrends* we wrote "trends, like horses, are easier to ride in the direction they are already going." This is certainly true when it comes to trends that have already become part of a mainstream technology, business practice, philosophy or ideology. But to leverage the opportunities of an evolving new world, we need to be with the frontrunners, and not the last in the queue. Mastering megatrends is very much linked to the willingness to adapt your mind to when new information is available.

You Can't Make an Omelet Without Breaking An Egg

The old French proverb is simple. A cook can't keep the eggs and make an omelet and the egg cannot be part of an omelet without being broken.

We can create change and change can be imposed on us. We can stand up for our own idea or we can follow the idea of others. We can show resistance or check the facts. When we are in fear to be proven wrong or too stubborn to deal with contradictive opinions we are limiting ourselves as if we would walk in hedged lanes. But once we experience the power of not having to be right we take the hedges down, allow our perspectives to widen and free ourselves to take any turn.

On record forever

It has never been possible to take back what we once said. But it used to be easier to make a misconduct forgotten. Today there is little space to hide. Every word said can be recorded; every move made can be filmed, multiplied in the web and in social networks. All opinions can be published, confirmed and contradicted.

At the same time access to information is easier than it has ever been. And so is the danger to be disgraced by false allegation. Humans are able to close their eyes against the most evident facts if they do not match the frozen pictures in their heads.

The history of science is a history full of resistance broken. In the section about education, we wrote about Einstein and how without scientific imagination he could have never stood up against the scientific establishment of his time. But it took more than that. He needed to stand up against his own education, against mainstream thinking and most of all, against of the worldwide scientific establishment. Looking back it may seems that this was easy for a genius like him. At the time though he did so without any signal of a genius breakthrough, but with all signs towards failure when his dissertation was turned down.

Stand up for *what* is right, not *who* is right

Einstein was convinced "authority slavery is one of the biggest enemies of truth." He paid for it by not finding a job in academic fields, despite sending stacks of applications. After an intermission as a teacher in the sleepy Swiss town of Schaffhausen he was hired as patent examiner in Bern.

Almost everyone is familiar with Einstein as the theoretical physicist whose theory of relatively and quantum theory have become pillars of modern physics. But few know the young man we get to know in his letters, the young Albert who worked with persistence but with the uncertainty and worry that he could take a wrong turn. In September 1911 he wrote to William Julius:

> "Highly esteemed Colleague,
>
> "If these [solar spectral] lines are very fine, then I believe that my theory is refuted by these observations. I would be very pleased if you told me candidly your opinion about this matter. After all, I know very well that my theory rests on a shaky foundation. The road I took might be the wrong one, but it had to be tried out."

Little more than 1 year later he still believed his idea was not only captivating, but also funny, wondering "if God is going to laugh because he was jokingly misleading me." He wrote to another acquaintance, astrophysicist Erwin Freundlich:

> "My theoretical studies are progressing briskly after indescribably painstaking research, so that the chances are good that the equations

for the general dynamics of the gravitation will be set up soon. The beauty of the thing is that one can keep clear of arbitrary assumptions, so that there is nothing to be 'patched up'; instead, the whole thing will be either true or false."

Substance instead of ego

To stand up and overturn established concepts of time and space sound much easier looking back to the Einstein we know as global celebrity. The foundation of his breakthrough was to stand up for what was right, not who was right.

One of Einstein's biographers, Albrecht Fössling, even speculated it might have been an advantage that "a man of such condition did not bother to get entangled in discussions with leading scientists, but was hanging out with his thoughts in his own diaspora."

To master megatrends does not take the genius and bravery of Einstein's mind. But surrounded by mass media, social networks with their echo chambers and living in a wall-to-wall information world it is much harder to hang out in a self-chosen diaspora. Even as we focus on substance and facts it is easy to underestimate the influence mainstream thinking on our own decision-making processes.

Surround yourself with optimists

We cannot choose the environment we are born into. But as we grow older we can choose with whom we surround ourselves. And once in a while it is helpful to reflect on with whom we spend our time. Do you surround yourself by people who are pessimistic and negative spirited or positive and optimistic? Sometimes we are not aware of how much harm the influence of a negative person can have on what we do and how we think. But if it comes to media we almost have no choice. Media's credo "only bad news is news" is supporting an atmosphere stricken with apprehension. Trained by a daily diet of local and global collections of calamities and problems, we look at the world with worry. Our mental roadmap is lined with flashing lights and warning signs cautioning us not to turn into the unknown and then blaming us for inaction if we didn't.

When the wish is the father to the thought

When it comes to judgments about economic, political and social developments there is no need to turn into the unknown. But there is the necessity to look at what is going on right now as unbiased as possible which, given the biased reporting, is not such an easy goal. We are very negatively impressed in how obsolete pictures of various countries are. The list once more led by opinions about China, which are reaching from: Do you have to take your own food with you? Can you even walk on the streets with all the people living in China? Other countries, for example Brazil, raise pictures of the Carnival in Rio, Copacabana beach and good-looking girls and hardly dirty and crowded streets in Sao Paulo. Desolate buildings in Italy are considered charming while the same conditions in other countries are judged as a sign of decline.

Seeing what we want to see rather than what is stands in the way. Who would have believed that people in the US could ever fall for Donald Trump, believing he made a U-turn from a perky philanderer to a caring philanthropist? One would think that the disappointment in politicians, the disillusion of promises made and never kept, the gridlock of the established system would sharpen the view on promises made. Instead it seems the most outrageous, implausible fantasy of a candidate hitting the sweet spot of wishful thinking of potential voters is more successful than any rational solution-oriented analysis of a situation.

As opportunist and right-wing politicians and sensation-seeking mass media like turn to fear as an effective instrument of manipulation, we should keep the Greek philosophers Sophocles words in mind: "No enemy is worse than a bad adviser."

Today's Disruptions can be Tomorrow's Solutions

A fear fed by media and politicians is the uncertainty about what will happen to the huge number of rather unskilled people working in manufacturing. Looking into the future we cannot factor in what is not yet foreseeable.

We can take it as given that digitalization and Artificial Intelligence will lead to fundamental change. But we cannot predict whether and which invention or innovation may be so disruptive that it leads to another, yet unknown turn. That's why struggling with problems only helps when it concerns fixing something that can be fixed, machines, roads, houses, cars and sometimes even relationships. If we look back in history, the solutions came often from unexpected and unforeseeable sources. It is as if we entered a one-way road, if we want to change directions, we have to switch to another road.

London 1880s: Different trigger, same basics

An example of "another road taken" goes back 240 years. Picture yourself to be living in London in the 1880s. London's city is growing and buzzing. To meet all the demands, around 50,000 horses are transporting people and goods around the city of London each day. That might sound romantic today, but it had its problems.

With such numbers of horse carriages London's roads were getting crowded and people, just like today's are suffering from heavy traffic. But the even darker and smelly side for the city was that horses produce manure and urine. Tons of manure and urine were polluting the air and the roads. And not very different from todays gloomy stories, mainstream media were predicting a very inglorious scenario. London's newspaper *The Times* raised one of the warning voices of the looming disaster: "The Horse Manure Crisis."

The prediction was based on solid and growing grounds: each of London's 50,000 horses produced between 15 and 35 pounds of manure per day, plus two pints of urine. Given those facts, people were not surprised to read *The Times's* prediction: "In 50 years, every street in London will be buried under nine feet of manure." The only ones who looked at the bright side of the development were London's blacksmiths, as more manure means more horses to clean and more horseshoes to be replaced.

The disruptive invention of Karl Benz

The situation though was not limited to London. While blacksmiths were experiencing their heydays, nearly every major city struggled with the same waste disposal issue. New York had as many as 100,000 horses producing 2.5 million pounds of manure per day! Not different than today, the American government wanted the issue to be debated at the first Urban Planning Conference in New York held in 1898. Similar to today, the conference ended without a solution. The problem of mountains of the manure remained even though we can be sure that many agonized over how it could be solved.

Looking back it might just cause us a smile. We know what happened. While mainstream media was busy predicting gloom and doom scenarios, the unpredicted solution was already in the works, not so far away by Karl Benz in Germany.

Karl Benz was not seeking to solve the problem of too much manure. And neither were the other inventors involved in the process of creating a motorized vehicle. They picked up the pieces of various inventions that made the construction of automobiles possible. Patents were filed, the automobile was invented, but way too expensive for the average person. It was Henry Ford's first moving assembly line which did not only increase productivity eightfold, but also made cars easily affordable. People could travel and transport their goods with motorcars.

The result solved the problem of the horse manure, not achieved by trying to solve the problem, but by an invention seeking to revolutionize transportation.

And not everyone embrace the invention. Still in disbelieve and resistance, in 1903, the President of the Michigan Savings Bank advised Horace Rackham, Henry Ford's lawyer, not to invest in the Ford Motor Co: "The horse is here to stay but the automobile is only a novelty — a fad."

Brian Groom reflected on it in an article in the *Financial Times* in September 2013: "The London Manure Crisis is also an example of humanities inability to foresee how economic incentives can produce technological solutions to a problem."

The Churning of Jobs

The big picture of transport had changed to the better, even though now the blacksmiths, whose profession had been in place for almost 2000 years, were getting in trouble. Those who focused on the problem might have tried to offer better horseshoes, worked more and harder and hoped the cars won't make it. Those who looked for new opportunities might have pushed towards using their qualities in different ways. And true enough, close to the basic material automobiles were built of, blacksmiths became the first generation of automobile mechanics.

The churning of jobs has been with us for a long time and is in fact contributing to growth. Nevertheless churning of jobs is not sustained or supported by the attempt to hold on to obsolete methods of production.

Let's take American factory workers uncertain about keeping their jobs. The US is still ranking number two in the global competitive index of manufacturing. But 2015 labor costs per hour were $37.96 on average. Compare that with China, which ranks number one in the index and labor costs per hour of $3.28. Or India, which ranks 11 but has labor costs of only $1.72 per hour. How safe is the manufacturing environment?

You can argue that a factory can raise productivity, made in USA is of higher value, technological standards are stricter and so forth. Improvements are possible, but the core problem remains and that is the changing context in which manufacturing takes place. It is not only cheap labor in emerging economies that feed uncertainty, but increasing automation, artificial intelligence and digital production that will wipe out many traditional production models. The US will remain competitive in the index, and even gain back its number one ranking but fewer and fewer people will find work in manufacturing jobs.

Keeping your mind on a problem, factory workers feel they are hit by three crises: the possible loss of the specific job, the fading of the manufacturing environment, and the changing global context for manufacturing. Positive thinking factory workers will accept the unchangeable and start looking for other opportunities as it will be clear that no matter how hard they work only a small number of them will remain in the blue color labor market. The solution is not how to fix assembly lines but to find opportunities elsewhere.

The Biggest Potatoes Cannot Bring Back Pre-industrial Days

A good example that situations mostly are not as gloomy as they seem at the beginning of a transition were related to farmers who faced the turn from an agricultural society to industrial society. Millions of jobs in most countries of the world were and are lost and the biggest potatoes and hardest work could not change that. If we look at statistics there was a rapid decline of labor force working in agriculture with a big drop beginning in 1800, which has not come to a stop.

The challenge returned as countries began transforming from industrial to information societies. The demand for professional workers has gained substantially since 1960, even more dramatically than the rising need for clerical workers.

In 1960 the approximately 7.5 million professional workers were the fifth largest job category and employed about 11 percent of the workforce.

In 1979, the number-one occupation in the United States, numerically, became clerk, succeeding laborer, and succeeding farmer. By 2012, that number had nearly quadrupled to 27.7 million professional and technical employees in the US representing about 20 percent of the overall workforce (Department for Professional Employees, AFL-CIO). Today the second largest classification after clerk is professional, completely in tune with the new information society, where knowledge is the critical ingredient.

How likely is it that America or any other country can solve the job loss problem in manufacturing? Can countries raise trade tax for imports of emerging economies? Yes, they can. Can they give orders to companies to make a step back and "manufacture in the old way" as Mr. Trump announced during his campaign? Hardly. In addition, what would be the impact on Americans who then would have to pay much more for US made products? Who will jump in and pay the difference?

It sounds absurd that the country, which for such a long period has been the driver of technological progress, would now seek solutions in turning to the past. Ironically at a time when its largest challenger does exactly the opposite, calling for becoming an innovation nation. America has and hopefully will remain an opportunity seeker and move on.

Opportunity-oriented people peel off

What's hardly possible in the US for some time has been tried out in some autocratic countries. But as Venezuela's President Maduro's failed "socialist" politics show rowing against the stream of time and economic developments can only work for a very short time.

China's autocratic government on the other hand is well aware that they have to do the opposite of holding on to the past, namely get ahead of the parade to sustain necessary economic growth. Already in 1990 President Jiang Zemin said in a private meeting with one of the authors, John, that the biggest challenge China was facing at the time was laying off blue color workers in non-productive factories. At that time mostly State Owned Enterprises (SOEs), today it is true in all industries.

Thanks to the enormous size of the country and the different stages of economic development, from underdeveloped to highly developed, China's blue color workforce has been able to move to where new factories needed workforce. But that migration will slowly come to an end within the next two decades. Opportunity-oriented people are already peeling off, seeking their fortune in other job categories.

To look back in history helps to get away from emotions and put things into a larger and less personal perspective. Think of the various opinions about globalization. Globalization was not a decision made by interest groups or governments. It is not a development one could make and discard again. Globalization was the consequence of developments in technology, production, trade, transportation and communication. Whether we are in favor or dismissive of globalization, the "economic game" has changed. How significant the role employees, entrepreneurs and enterprises play within that development depends on their flexibility to adjust and reinvent.

Turning to Those Who Should Know

In his 1919 book *The Economic Consequences of the Peace*, John Maynard Keynes, the great economist predicted that the wounds of war struck in Germany would be extended by the reparation payments. He had participated in the negotiations of the peace treaty of Versailles after WWI, and strongly disagreed with the high war reparations imposed on Germany. Looking at the facts he was pre-alerted about events that eventually really happened: the reparations required of Germany led to catastrophe of WWII. Comprehensible today but rejected and denied for various reasons at the time.

Or take Friedrich Hayek, the Austrian economist who in his 1945 book *The Use of Knowledge in Society* predicted the collapse of Communism. And he did so for a solid reason: successful central governing would need to know the decisions made by the market before they are made, which of course is impossible.

In 1961 Paul Samuelson contradicted that statement heavily. Samuelson, who was the first American to win the first Nobel Prize in economics in 1970, said that "the Soviet economy is proof that contrary to what many sceptics had earlier believed, a socialist command can function and even thrive." He was not the only Economist who got things wrong.

The tolerance towards Economist's predictions is rather high

Joan Robinson, a British economist well known for her work on monetary economics and wide ranging economic theories, and not surprisingly one of the most promising economists of the 20th century, said after visiting the Koreas, which had been separated since

1945, in 1964 that "as the North continues to thrive and the South to degenerate, soon or later the curtain of lies must begin to tear."

A prediction he probably was loved for and even loved much more if it had come true was made much earlier by Irving Fisher, one of America's great economists. In October 1929, two weeks before Wall Street Crash on "Black Tuesday," he announced that he was convinced that equities had reached a "permanently high plateau." It took 25 years to regain what was lost.

The book *Japan As Number One* was released by Ezra Vogel, a Harvard Social Scientist in 1976. He predicted that the United States Economy would soon be surpassed by Japan.

How hard it is to get it right even if you are chief investment strategist of Goldman Sachs was proven by Abby Joseph Cohen in December 2007. She suggested the S&P 500 would hit 1,675 by the end of 2008. But instead of the climb by 14 percent, it ended below 900, almost half of its value predicted.

Anyone would have been happy if James Glassman, founding director of the George W. Bush Institute, and Kevin Hasset, and American economist, would have been at least half right with their 1999 prediction that the Dow Jones would triple from its height of 11,497 in the coming years to reach 36,000. Even 16 years later it has not even doubled.

The Age of Turbulence was the title of Alan Greenspan's 2007 book in which he warned that the world might need double digit interest rates to control inflation in the near future. China's interest rate peaked in 2008 and came to a low of little more than 4 percent in 2016. In the US and Europe interest rates have been near zero for the past years.

George Soros, worth almost $25 billion, estimated that the Chinese inflation was "somewhat out of control" in 2011 with a danger of sprawling further. On the other hand, his family office made almost $1 billion from November 2012 to February 2013 betting that the Japanese Yen would tumble under Shinzo Abe.

Ravi Batra, an Indian-American economist earned the laurels of writing a *New York Times* Number One bestseller, but to be right on what it said was another matter. *Surviving the Great Depression of 1990* gave an outlook to great turmoil. But in fact the 1990s became a period of extended global growth.

And let's end with sunny-boy billionaire Richard Branson who in 2010 issued a warning of a severe oil shortage: "the next five years will see us face another crunch — the oil crunch." Six years later the price is lower than it was then.

That list of course leaves us with the question to whom to turn to.

Holding on to reliable sources

Of course, anyone who talks or writes about coming developments can go wrong. The less available the reliable information is, the riskier is any estimate. Developments on larger scales are easier to monitor while, for example, currency swings or stock market moves carry high risk and the lurking danger of irrational moves.

So how can you master megatrends, if you fear the information available is not reliable. Stay away from personal opinions. Look at the facts.

Think of newspapers. If you love sports and read the newspaper back to front you are starting with the most reliable part. Results, goals and records are hardly ever reported incorrectly. Less so when it comes to opinions about certain plays and players. Same is true of course with blogs, but at least they do not come in disguise.

There is no certainty in what will happen, but we can, with some effort, get a decent picture of the present. Once we have that, the question "what comes next?" will be based on the solid grounds of the directions presented now by facts and not by wishful thinking.

Differentiate between trends and fads

There is in addition a large difference between what's commonly called trends and a real megatrend. What often is called a trend or even a megatrend is mostly afad. Consumer trends are a good example and while they are important for most industries their impact is not sustainable. They come and go. Trends are developments and behaviors that evolve and become permanent. Megatrends can be based on individual inventions and innovations, and the unfolding of social-economic change, like the information society and the globalization of our economies.

Nevertheless, to master megatrends will sometimes hold the need reach out for the opportunity even if the picture is still foggy and the context in which it is hidden remains hidden to us. Not because someone is hiding it but because we are so focused on our problems that we do not even dare to lift the curtain and look for opportunities.

Not in Fear to be Wrong

Mastering our thoughts, keeping them as independent as possible and holding on to our intuition is not always easy, but important to us. Of course we can go wrong. In the period between 2000 and 2005, we were convinced the US would remain a hegemon for some decades. Even though we were in China several times each year we underestimated the speed in which it developed and the strategic moves it was already making, which looking back have become obvious.

And, we must add, we overestimated the ability of the US to regenerate and certainly the desperation of the people, which allowed someone like Trump to fool them.

The path of stagnation in the EU though was becoming apparent rather soon, but very unpopular early as the EU did not hold back with self-praise. The drama of the EU is that it would like to have the economic and political power a "United States of Europe" could hold, but dislikes all it would take to get there.

In the beginning of this book, we said that the most frequent question we get is the question for the next megatrend, mostly followed by the next popular; How many times did you go wrong? In case you have the same questions in mind, here is a summary of key statements in the books:

1982 *Megatrends*
   Industrial Society to Information Society
   National Economy to World Economy
   Hierarchies to Networking

1990 *Reinventing the Corporation*
Social trends and information technology will influence corporate behavior
The computer will substitute mid-level jobs Mature corporations will nurture intra-entrepreneurship

1992 *Megatrends for Women*
Women, yet not fully liberated, are building a new social order
Women will break through top corporate posts
Upsurge of women in politics

1994 *Megatrends Asia*
What is happening in Asia is by far the most important development in the world today. Nothing else comes close, not only for Asians but for the entire planet. The modernization of Asia will forever reshape the world as we move towards the next millennium

2000 *High Tech High Touch*
Technology as the currency of our lives is as much a benefit as it is a trap. Technology Intoxicated Zones like video games in which children suck up violence, the dangers of what's feasible in biotech industries.
Internet is a social phenomenon

2006 *Mindset*
Europe is on a path to mutually assured decline
From nation states to economic domains

2010 *China's Megatrends*
Emancipating the minds
Crossing the river by feeling the stones
From Olympic Gold to Nobel laurels

2015 *Global Game Change*
From westerncentric to multicentric
The rise of the Global Southern Belt
China the game changer
Cities the global game makers

When a wish became the mother of a book

The megatrend, which is still in a waiting position to come, is *Megatrends for Women,* published in 1992 (John Naisbitt and

Patricia Aburdene). Even though in some countries women have gained ground, we are far away from gender equality. Of the total of 579 Nobel Prizes and Economic Science Prize awarded between 1901 and 2016, only 48 women were chosen.

No gender equality in our lifetime

The latest World Economic Forum report on gender equality describes the gap larger than in 2006, in part because of specific issues in China and India. Their (very theoretical) estimate in how many years gender gaps would narrow paints a gloomy picture: Asia leads with 46 years, Western Europe 61 years, Latin America in 72 years, Sub Sahara Africa 79 years. East Asia and the Pacific is calculated with 146 years, Eastern Europe and Central Asia might be able to celebrate gender equality in 149 years. And the US? An American dream of closing the gap might come true in 158 years. The leaders are Iceland, Finland, Norway, Sweden, and strikingly Rwanda at 5th and Philippines at 7th positions.

Women are still the minority in leading positions. The percentage of business leadership roles held by women:

Globally, women hold only 24 percent of senior business roles.

One-third of all companies have no women at all in senior positions.

The two worst countries regarding the percentage in women holding senior positions are Japan with 7 percent, and Germany 15 percent.

In India 2016, women held 16 percent of senior leadership roles.

Eastern Europe has 35 percent, and ASEAN 34 percent women in leading positions.

And 16 percent of Eastern Europe's and 21 percent of ASEAN companies report no women in senior management.

China 30 percent of women made it into in leading positions.

On top of the list surprisingly (to us) Russia, with 45 percent of leading positions held by women.

Followed by the (as surprising) Philippines at 39 percent (*Grant Thornton Research* published in 2015).

In Korea women have surpassed men in university entrance but they are still underrepresented in many elite fields: only 19 percent of all lawyers, 23.9 percent of doctors, and 23 percent of university professors. Of the 46 percent women who passed the civil service exam only 8.8 percent made it into civil service positions.

The number of women on boards of Indian companies has increased. Credit Suisse' Gender 3000 Report for 2016 reaffirmed "that its prior findings that companies with higher participation of women in decision-making roles continue to generate higher market returns and superior profits."

Nevertheless, Tina Vinod of Thought Works India indicated: "Unfortunately, the systemic patriarchy and unconscious bias in our (India's) culture continues to seep into the workforce. The leaking pipeline of potential women leaders is a huge concern."

The disadvantage to be born female: Not mastered at all

Even though most children are better off than ever, in many parts of the world, including Western countries, we still see too much gender inequity. With reference to the "Day of the Girl" 2016, German DIE ZEIT reported some examples of lack of freedom and education, and suffering of violence. Each ninth girl is forced to marry before her 15th birthday. Fifteen million girls cannot even attend elementary school. Of the 780 million people illiterate people in the world almost two-thirds are women. Three quarters of the people living in poverty are women. Many of them raising their children as single mothers.

It was a disappointment to go wrong and hope for a faster change to more gender equality, which, despite all lip service, is not in sight. But as one of us, Doris, is a member of the International Women's Forum, we at least have a voice in an organization eager to contribute to Women's Megatrends.

Life is not fair

Despite all negative news on a global scale mankind is better off than ever. But in the same level we are better off, personal demands have risen. There is nothing wrong with that. But in a lot of "inequality" talks, in a lot of talk about the need for redistribution of wealth — hypocritical arguments can be found. Political correctness in language is used as a curtain to cover up underlying causes no one wants to touch.

The unshakable starting point is that life itself is not fair. We are born into different conditions. A great country, a poor country, supportive or neglecting parents, wealthy or poor, born with out-standing talent or average gifted. And while it is understandable that to live through unfair conditions in a disadvantageous envi-ronment can be frustrating, the worse we can do is slipping into a victim mentality.

Mastering megatrends by making the most of what we have

We cannot choose the environment to be born into, but we can choose what we make of what we have got victim mentality finds a million arguments why this and that is not possible. And there are regions and situations where the frame of personal freedom reached zero. But we are not talking about such conditions. We are talking about people like you and us.

Why would blue-color workers be the only "hard working" class? To those who want to achieve wealth the path is long working hours and high performance. Not everybody has the ability, not everybody wants to invest all it takes. Ambition must come from inside and cannot be imposed. It's we who decide which path to take.

Printed in the United States
By Bookmasters